Windows 95
hard disc and file management

OTHER BOOKS OF INTEREST

Windows 95 hard disc and file management

by
Jim Gatenby

BERNARD BABANI (publishing) LTD
THE GRAMPIANS
SHEPHERDS BUSH ROAD
LONDON W6 7NF
ENGLAND

PLEASE NOTE

Although every care has been taken with the production of this book to ensure that any projects, designs, modifications and/or programs, etc., contained herewith, operate in a correct and safe manner and also that any components specified are normally available in Great Britain, the Publishers and Author do not accept responsibility in any way for the failure (including fault in design) of any project, design, modification or program to work correctly or to cause damage to any equipment that it may be connected to or used in conjunction with, or in respect of any other damage or injury that may be so caused, nor do the Publishers accept responsibility in any way for the failure to obtain specified components.

Notice is also given that if equipment that is still under warranty is modified in any way or used or connected with home-built equipment then that warranty may be void.

First Published - March 1998

British Library Cataloguing in Publication Data:

A catalogue record for this book is available from the
British Library

ISBN 0 85934 4452

Cover Design by Gregor Arthur
Cover illustration by Adam Willis
Printed and bound in Great Britain by Cox & Wyman Ltd, Reading

ABOUT THIS BOOK

This book is written for the Windows 95 user who has neither the time nor the inclination to get too deeply involved in the technicalities of computing. Its aim is to provide a good understanding of the ways to manage the hard disc efficiently, with much emphasis on the safety and protection of its contents.

A knowledge of the management of files and folders is essential for all serious Windows 95 users and this is covered at the beginning of the book. With increasing use of the Internet and its integration within the Windows desktop, the handling of Internet files cannot be ignored. The Internet is now a major source of software, data files and e-mail sent direct to your hard disc and the implications of this are discussed at length in the first half of the book.

Many people quickly grasp the basics of producing and saving documents, but little attention is paid to safeguarding what often amounts to weeks or months of hard work. A moment's carelessness or a virus can easily wipe out priceless data and program files. Sensible back up procedures remove the worry of these potential disasters. Later chapters describe how this security can be achieved at a modest cost in relation to the value of your hard disc files.

Windows 95 provides tools needed to keep the hard disc free from errors and performing at its optimum. These maintenance tools are described in detail, together with an overview of some of the most popular accessories available from third party companies, such as file compression and anti-virus software.

Some readers may prefer to work through certain sections at the computer; alternatively you can dip into the book to get a quick understanding of many of today's most pertinent topics.

ABOUT THE AUTHOR

Jim Gatenby trained as a Chartered Mechanical Engineer and initially worked at Rolls-Royce Ltd using mainframe computers in the analysis of gas turbine performance. He obtained a Master of Philosophy degree in Mathematical Education by research at Loughborough University of Technology and has taught mathematics and computing to 'A' Level since 1972. His most recent posts have included Head of Computer Studies and IT Manager. During this time he has written several books in the field of educational computing and was involved in the pilot studies on the first wide area networks in education, before the arrival of the Internet.

TRADEMARKS

CONTENTS

1. FILES AND FOLDERS

Introduction

This section gives an overview of the way Windows 95 can be used to organise your work into a hierarchy of files and folders.

The term file, in this context, refers to a single piece of work stored on the hard disc, such as a letter or report, a spreadsheet, a drawing or a set of records from a database.

In the same way that loose papers in the traditional office are organised into folders, computer files are grouped into metaphorical folders on the hard disc. This makes it easier to find a particular piece of work. Disc management tasks such as copying or deleting groups of files are much simpler. Folders are a graphical representation of the *directories* used in earlier systems. The terms are otherwise synonymous.

Windows 95 provides two ways of managing files and folders; Windows Explorer and My Computer.

The Windows Explorer

The Explorer is opened using **Start, Programs** and **Explorer.**

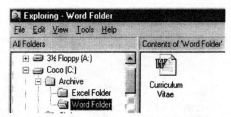

Explorer is particularly useful for viewing the hierarchical or branching structure of the disc and its folders. Folders are opened up to reveal the sub-folders and files within.

My Computer

 This is started by double clicking on its icon on the Windows Desktop.

My Computer gives an immediate view of the different disc storage devices and the control panel and printer(s). In addition to file management tasks, My Computer is also used for setting up new hardware and software.

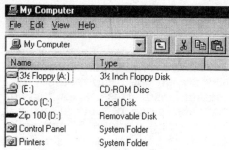

The folders on the hard disc drive, Coco(C:) in this case, are revealed by double clicking on its icon.

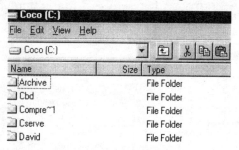

Both the Windows Explorer and My Computer can be used for managing files and folders, either by "dragging" and "dropping" with the mouse or by using the menus accessed from **File** and **Edit**. These tasks are covered in detail in later sections.

The Folder "My Documents"

My Documents

Windows 95 is designed to simplify the organisation of your work into folders; so when you save a new piece of work it will be placed, by default, into a folder called **My Documents**. (Unless you have selected a different folder).

Opening up the folder **My Documents** on my particular computer, as shown in the window below, illustrates that a folder can contain various types of file, indicated by their different icons.

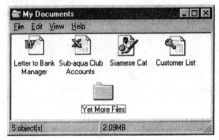

The file types shown above are:

- A Word document
- An Excel spreadsheet
- A picture from Paint
- An Access database file

The Hierarchy of Folders

The above window for the folder My Documents also contains another folder within it - a "sub-folder"- in this example called **Yet More Files**. This idea of folders within folders is illustrated in the Windows Explorer in which the branching or hierarchical structure is clearly displayed. This can be seen by selecting **Start, Programs** and **Explorer**.

3

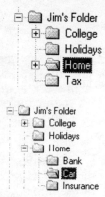

The screen shot on the left shows my main folder with 4 sub-folders branching off. The + sign indicates that a folder contains more folders within it.

Clicking on the + sign against the folder **Home** reveals three sub-folders, **Bank**, **Car** and **Insurance.** (Clicking the - sign to the left of **Home** hides the sub-folders **Bank**, **Car** and **Insurance**).

The files contained in the folder **Car** are revealed in the Windows Explorer by clicking on the folder icon.

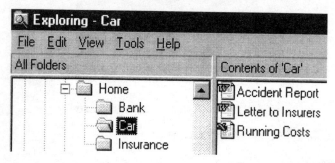

It can be seen that the folder **Car** contains 3 files, two Word documents and an Excel spreadsheet. Note that, unlike previous Windows versions, Windows 95 allows files to be saved with longer and more meaningful file names such as "Running Costs".

You can also view the contents of a folder in My Computer. This shows the files in their own window, but you do not see the hierarchy of folders and sub-folders as you do in the Windows Explorer.

Files in Detail

We have seen that files are at the bottom of the organisational hierarchy. There are two main categories of file; program files and data files.

Program Files

These files make up the software applications such as Microsoft Office and Windows 95 itself. Normally the user will have no reason to modify or delete these files except when upgrading to later versions. Program files have extensions like .EXE and .DLL, and should be left well alone.

Data Files

These cover everything you produce, ranging from wordprocessing text, database and spreadsheet files, to pictures and music - all often referred to as "documents". You will be concerned with creating, editing and organising your data files.

Types of Data File

When a file is created, e.g. by saving in one of the applications, such as Word, an icon is attached to indicate the type of file.

The icons above represent files created in Word, Access, Excel and Paint respectively. If a program does not create its own specific icon, the general-purpose Windows 95 icon, as shown on the right, is attached.

The details of files, such as their size and type, can be seen in the Windows Explorer by selecting the required sub-folder and then choosing **View** and **Details**.

Contents of 'Car'			
Name	Size	Type	Modified
Accident Report	11KB	Microsoft Word Doc...	7/29/97 11:
Letter to Insurers	11KB	Microsoft Word Doc...	7/29/97 11:
Running Costs	15KB	Microsoft Excel Wor...	7/29/97 11:

Filename Extensions

Although Windows 95 doesn't normally display them, files are saved with a 3-letter extension which identifies the file type. For example, program files are saved with the **.EXE** extension. In the text-only MSDOS system which preceded the icon-based Windows system, extensions were the only way of displaying the file type. You can see the MSDOS extensions in Windows 95 by selecting the required folder in Explorer or My Computer, then selecting **View**, **Options** and switching off **Hide MS-DOS file extensions....**

This dialogue box also allows you to hide certain types of file, such as those with the **.DLL** extension, for example.

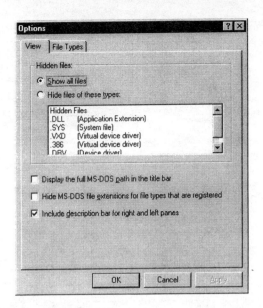

The extract from the Windows Explorer below shows the .doc extension given to Word documents and the .xls extension which is used for Excel spreadsheets.

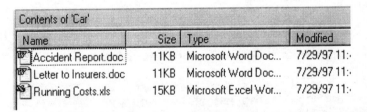

Windows 95 keeps a list of registered file types. This list can be examined (and modified) in either My Computer or Explorer, using **View**, **Options** and **File Types.**

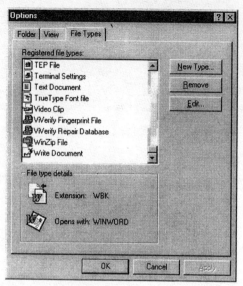

The dialogue box shows the registered file types, including their icons, their filename extension and the program which can be used to open them.

File Properties

When a file is saved, it is given certain properties and attributes by default. The user may view the default properties in My Computer or the Windows Explorer.

To view a file's properties, first click the icon to the left of the filename. The filename should be surrounded by a coloured background. Then select **File** and a menu appears which includes, amongst others, the option to display the file **Properties.**

Selecting **Properties** allows you to view the details and change the file attributes if necessary.

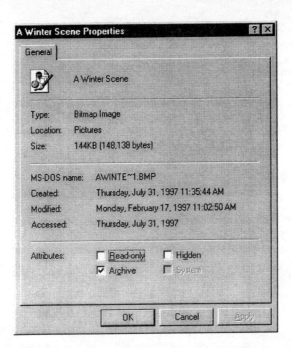

The **Properties** dialogue box above shows the icon attached to the file by Windows 95 - in this case a Paint file. It also shows that the file is a Bitmap Image with the .BMP extension.

The truncated MS-DOS name AWINTE~1.BMP shows how MSDOS can only handle filenames of up to 8 characters (compared with the full name "A Winter Scene" which Windows 95 displays). At the bottom of the properties dialogue box, are the file attributes **Read-Only**, **Hidden**, **Archive** and **System**. The tick boxes to the left allow the attributes to be switched on or off.

Switching these attributes on with a tick has the following effects:

Read Only

This attribute would be switched on to protect important files which you don't want deleted (either accidentally or deliberately). You can view the contents of the file but the file cannot be altered or deleted.

Hidden

Files which you wish to remain confidential can be protected by switching this attribute on. Anyone else using the computer will not be aware of the existence of hidden files. The filename will not appear when you view the contents of folders using the Windows Explorer or My Computer or when you do **File**, **Open** to reveal a list of files in an application such as Word. To open a hidden file, you need to know the filename and type it in during a **File**, **Open** operation.

To make sure your "hidden" files really are hidden you need to set My Computer or the Windows Explorer using **View**, **Options**, **View** and **Hide files of these types.**

Archive

As discussed in the section on backing up files, you may only wish to back up certain files. If the archive attribute is ticked, the file will be backed up or archived next time the hard disc is backed up.

System

System files are essential for the operation of the computer. Most users will not be concerned with system files and no attempt should be made to alter or delete them.

Managing Files and Folders

This section deals with the common tasks involved in managing your folders and the files you have produced in Word, Excel, Access, etc. These tasks include saving your work in different folders and on different discs. Also copying, moving, deleting and renaming files and folders. As much of this work is accomplished using the mouse, some of the main mouse skills are listed below:

Basic Mouse Skills

Single Click the **left** hand mouse button:

- Highlight a file or folder prior to copying, moving or deleting etc.

- Select an option from a menu.

Single Click the **right** hand mouse button to:

- Access various menus which are relevant to where the mouse happens to be pointing at the time.

Double Click the **left** hand mouse button to:

- Open up a disc drive or folder in its own window, showing the folders and files within.

- Start a program e.g. invoking My Computer from its icon on the desktop.

"**Dragging**" and "**dropping**" involves selecting an item with the left (or right) mouse button then, without releasing the button, moving the cursor to a new location. The button is then released resulting in either the copying or moving of a file or folder. (Discussed in more detail later.)

11

Creating Files in a Specified Location

Selecting the Destination Disc

A file is created every time you save a piece of work you have produced in an application such as Word, Excel or Paint. Using the **Save As** option you can select the disc you want to save the work on. On my machine there is a choice of the C: drive (hard disc), the floppy disc in the A: drive or the removable hard disc (ZIP disc) in the D: drive. (Drive E: being the CD-ROM drive which is currently read-only on most, but not all, computers).

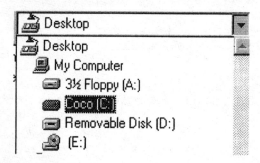

Selecting the Folder

When you have selected the disc on which to save your work, you then choose the target folder in which it is to be placed by opening up the main folder and highlighting the sub-folder.

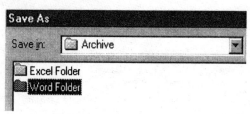

Adding the Filename

At this point you can enter the name you wish to give to the file. Windows 95 permits long filenames (up to 255 characters). So you can give the file a meaningful name which will help to identify it at a later date.

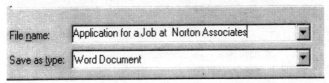

Although, by default, the computer will save the document as, for example, a Word file, it is possible to specify a different file type by selecting the option **Save as type**.

You might wish to save a document produced using Word and give it to a friend who uses a different program which can't import Word files. Saving as a **Text Only** file will produce a file (with a very basic format) which can be imported into a variety of software.

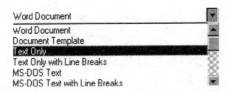

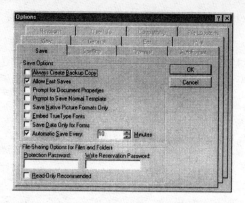

The **Automatic Save Every:** is a useful device. If set to 10 minutes, say, your work will be regularly saved to the hard disc while you are working, with minimal disturbance. Without regular saving there is a risk of losing all of the work, if a system crash or power cut occurs after a session lasting 2 hours, say.

The **Save As...** command also allows you to apply a password to prevent anyone else looking at the files.

Apart from any regular backup strategy you may be using (as discussed in later sections) it's very easy, while producing an important document, to make an extra copy (in addition to the hard disc copy) to a floppy disc as you are working. Use the **Save As...** option and select **3½ Floppy (A:)** as the destination.

Creating Folders

As with many Windows operations, there are several alternative ways to create a new folder. Both the Windows Explorer and My Computer can be used and the basic methods are very similar. I have chosen to use Explorer in this example since it shows the hierarchy of folders including folders within folders.

14

Suppose I want to start a new folder, **Building Project,** to hold files on some home improvements. I want to create the new folder within my existing folder **Home** which itself resides in **Jim's Folder** at the top level of the hierarchy under the C: drive.

Start the Windows Explorer and highlight the **Home** folder into which the new folder is to be located. Select **File**, **New** and **Folder** and a **New Folder** will appear as shown below. Alternatively you can press the right hand mouse button over an empty part of the Explorer right hand window, then select **New** and **Folder.**

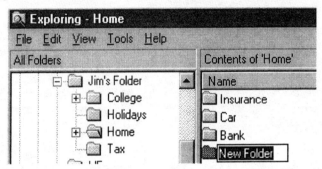

As can be seen above, the **New Folder** has been placed in the **Home** folder (shown open). The flashing cursor can be used to delete the default name **New Folder** and replace with the chosen name **Building Project.**

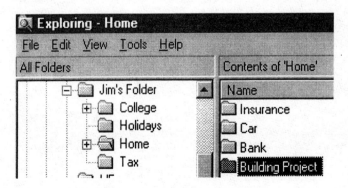

You can place new folders anywhere in your hierarchy provided the required "parent" folder which is to host the new folder is highlighted first. To place a new folder at the highest level, simply make sure that your **C:** drive name is highlighted before selecting **File**, **New** and **Folder**.

Renaming Files and Folders

This work can be carried out equally well in the Windows Explorer or in My Computer. As usual there are several alternative methods.

A folder or file can be re-named by clicking on its name with two distinctly separate clicks of the left mouse button. Or the folder or filename can be highlighted followed by selection of the menu options **File** and **Rename**. A further option is to highlight the folder or filename, press the right hand button over the name, then select **Rename** from the menu which appears.

The folder name or filename appears in a rectangle with a flashing cursor. Rename the folder or file by deleting the existing name and typing in the new one.

Deleting Files and Folders

The method for deleting files is the same as that for deleting folders. Select the file or folder in the Windows Explorer or My Computer so that its name is highlighted. Then either press the **Delete** key or select **Delete** from the **File** menu. If you have selected a folder to be deleted then all of the sub-folders and files contained within will also be deleted.

Unlike some earlier systems, Windows 95 doesn't require a folder to be empty before it can be deleted. If you make a mistake and delete the wrong folders or files, you can use the **Undo Delete** option in the **Edit** menu (provided you spot the mistake straight away.)

However, files are not lost forever when they are deleted. Windows 95 merely transfers them to its **Recycle Bin.**

The Recycle Bin

This is really just a folder into which all deleted files are sent. An easy way to delete files (in Explorer and My Computer) is to drag the icon for the file or folder and drop it over the Recycle Bin on the Windows Desktop.

You can view the contents of the Recycle Bin at any time by double clicking on its icon on the Desktop.

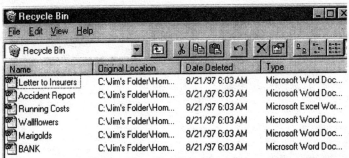

Files which have been "deleted" remain in the Recycle Bin until you decide to empty it. This is done by selecting **File** then **Empty Recycle Bin** off the menu bar at the top of the Recycle Bin window. The Recycle Bin should be emptied regularly to free up disc space.

Should you wish to reinstate files which have been consigned to the bin, open up the Recycle Bin window by double clicking on its icon. Then highlight the files to be restored and select **File** and **Restore** from the menu bar for the Recycle Bin. The files will be restored to their original locations.

WARNING !

It is extremely easy to move files and folders around a hard disc. However, these notes apply only to the manipulation of **data** files and folders which **you have created**.

Under no circumstances should you attempt to move or copy any of the **program files** or folders such as Windows, Office, Word, Excel, Access or any of the other applications. Windows expects to find the programs in specific locations and the effect of "tidying up" program files into your own folders will be to render the computer useless. (This does happen.)

N.B. Although the following tasks are described in the context of files, the notes apply equally to folders.

Moving a file deletes the file from its original location and places it in a new one.

Copying a file places an image of the file in a new location and leaves the original edition of the file in the original location.

Files may be copied or moved between different locations on the same hard disc or between different media such as hard and floppy discs.

The basic method is to drag the file or folder and drop it over the new location. Different results are obtained depending on whether you are dragging and dropping to the same or a different medium. The file is moved if your destination is the same hard disc or copied if the destination is a different disc. To copy files within the same hard disc the **Control** key must be held down while dragging with the left hand mouse button.

Using the Right Hand Mouse Button

If you drag the file icon using the right hand button on the mouse, when the button is released to drop the file over its new location, a menu appears. This allows you to select whether the file is to be moved or copied. This is probably the easiest and safest way of copying or moving files.

You can also copy and move files in My Computer by using the **Edit** menus in the respective windows. Select the file(s) then use **Edit** and either **Copy** or **Cut** in the first (source) window followed by **Edit** and **Paste** in the destination window.

Copying Multiple Files

Suppose you want to pick out a selection of files from within a folder and copy them to a floppy disc. This is done by opening two windows simultaneously in My Computer.

First open a window for the folder (**Temp** in this case) on the hard disc by double clicking on its icon. Then open the window for the floppy disc.

For ease of copying you can arrange for the two windows to appear together side-by-side on the screen. This is done by clicking the right hand button over the task bar at the bottom of the screen in My Computer. The menu shown right appears, giving options to arrange the windows in either horizontal or vertical tiling.

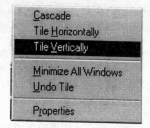

The screen shot below shows the window for the floppy disc (A:) alongside that of the Temp directory. (This arrangement was obtained by selecting **Tile Vertically**)

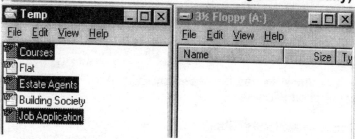

To select particular files, highlight them with the left hand button while simultaneously holding down the **Control** key. Then you can drag all of the files en bloc and drop them over the window for the floppy disc.

Caution ! Moving Files Can Be Dangerous

Great care is need when moving and copying to ensure that the desired operation is actually carried out. For example, if you mistakenly move (instead of copy) a group of files on to a floppy (perhaps to give someone else a copy), your own copies will no longer exist on the hard disc. Dragging with the right hand button then selecting copy or move from the resulting menu (described earlier) is probably the safest method.

Summary: Files and Folders

- A file is a piece of work which has been saved on a disc. Windows 95 permits filenames of up to 255 letters, so that meaningful names can be used.

- Files are created when you save your work in applications such as Word and Excel. These are generally referred to as documents or data files. Different applications produce different types of file identified with their own extension such as .doc or .xls

- The programs or applications which you run, such as Word and Excel, also contain files. These are known as program files (with extensions such as .exe) and these must not be moved, modified or deleted by the user.

- Windows 95 has been designed to allow the user to organise files easily into folders and sub-folders.

- Files have attributes which may be changed by the user. These include **Read Only** to prevent the file from being accidentally deleted, and **Hidden** to disguise the presence of the file. The **Archive** attribute marks the file as needing to be backed up.

- The Windows Explorer enables the folders, sub-folders and files to be viewed in their hierarchical branching structure.

- Both My Computer and the Windows Explorer provide facilities to manage your work including such tasks as creating folders, copying, moving, deleting and re-naming files and folders.

- The **Save As** option allows you to specify a particular destination for the file, including a particular folder or sub-folder and different disc drives like the hard disc, floppy disc or ZIP drive.

- Other options include the automatic saving of files at specified intervals, and the creation of a backup copy every time a file is saved.

- Files which are deleted are sent to the Windows Recycle Bin. They can still be restored to their original locations unless the option to empty the bin has been used. This should be done at regular intervals to preserve disc space.

- Most tasks can be accomplished by simple mouse operations either by "dragging" and "dropping" or selection from menus.

- The safest way to manipulate files and folders is to drag and drop with the right hand button then select the required copy or move operation from the menu which appears.

- Care should be taken when moving files: program files should never be moved. Accidental moving of files (when copying is intended) can result in the loss of important work from the original location.

2. CAPTURING INTERNET FILES

Introduction

The Internet is a myriad of linked computers spanning the entire globe in a network of networks. Many millions of these computers are used by ordinary people for activities like "surfing the net" or for sending and receiving e-mail. Machines used by the general public are known as **clients**.

Another category of computer is used to hold and distribute the files of information. These are known as host computers or **servers**. Currently there are over 19 million server machines worldwide and the number is increasing rapidly each year. Once on the Internet you therefore have the potential to "download" files from the hard discs on the servers on to your own hard disc. However, without sensible management your hard disc could easily be engulfed in a sea of downloaded files.

Improvements in communications technology with faster modems and digital ISDN lines continue to make the Internet more powerful, allowing the faster transmission of larger data files. These can include multimedia documents containing graphics, moving video and sound, as well as text and clip art.

Huge quantities of high quality software are freely available on the Internet - it is simply a matter of downloading to your hard disc. It is also possible, while sitting at a client machine, to run programs remotely at one of the servers, without the need to download the programs to the user or client machine.

Any use of the Internet will have important implications for your hard disc; you may choose to download software and data files which could rapidly fill the available disc space.

Even if you only use the Internet for browsing the World Wide Web, your surfing will result in a considerable amount of disc space being used. This is because Windows 95 automatically saves files needed for the efficient running of the system. (The files are saved in a cache or temporary store, in this case on the hard disc). The user will not normally encounter these files, but they are using valuable disc space which may be recoverable if they can safely be deleted

E-mail is one of the most important uses of the Internet and obviously generates a lot of files which can accumulate on your hard disc unless regularly managed.

Downloading Software - An Overview

It's possible to receive computer software transmitted over the Internet then stored on your hard disc. This is very fast and convenient compared with physically going to a shop and buying the software or sending for it by conventional mail order. Obviously you don't get the documentation and backup information as you do when buying a full package.

Sometimes the software is completely free with no strings attached. Both Microsoft and Netscape provide complete working copies of their Internet browser software free over the Internet.

Alternatively **shareware** is initially free but perhaps only for a limited evaluation period. Then you may be expected to pay for a registered version with full documentation and support. For example, it's possible to download an image viewing program called LView Pro. LView Pro can be obtained from:

http://www.lview.com/

When you run LView Pro you are given the choice of evaluating the software free for up to 21 days or you can buy a registered copy.

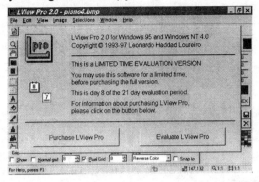

Many companies allow users to download advanced versions of software ("Beta" test copies). While accepting that, by definition, the beta test software may contain bugs which have still to be corrected, it's a useful way to obtain and evaluate the latest software.

All you have to do to download software is to connect to the Internet, locate the relevant Web site, then follow a few simple menus to download the files and install on to the hard disc. This is demonstrated in the next few pages by downloading a copy of the file compression program WinZip from the Internet.

Compressed Files

Before sending software over the Internet, it is compressed so that smaller and therefore faster packets of information can be transmitted. Increasingly files are converted to self-extractors before transmission. Then the compressed files are downloaded from the Internet into a folder on your hard disc.

Before the software can be installed and run it must be extracted or expanded. In the case of a self-extracting file, it is expanded by double-clicking on its name or icon in the Windows Explorer. Otherwise a program such as WinZip or PKUNZIP will have to be used for expanding the file.

Then the software must be installed or set up so that the program can actually run on your machine (in the same way that software is installed from floppies or CD).

Downloading a Copy of WinZip

WinZip is a file compression program and is discussed in detail later in this book. The software is freely available over the Internet, while a fully documented package is available through conventional suppliers. WinZip is particularly relevant to this chapter on Internet files since it can itself be used in the uploading and downloading process.

Starting the Download

First you need to know the URL (Uniform Resource Locator) or address of the Web page on the Internet where the software is located. If you first hear about the software in a magazine or newspaper article it should give the URL.

For WinZip, the Internet location is:

http://www.winzip.com/

Enter this URL into your Web browser such as Netscape or Internet Explorer.

If you don't know the URL of the Web site holding the software you should be able to find it by typing the name, in this case, "WinZip", into one of the well-known search engines such as Yahoo! or AltaVista.

Once you have located the Web site for the software a screen appears, giving a choice of the version of WinZip to download.

In this case the option **Download New Beta 6.3** was selected, revealing a further choice of version of Windows.

The download process is started by clicking over the hypertext link **Download WinZip 6.3 Beta** (selected when the pointer changes to a hand.)

You are then shown the folder into which the downloaded file is to be placed.

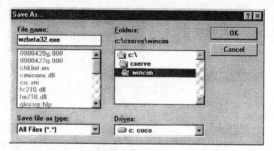

At this stage you can change the destination for the downloaded file by selecting a different folder in the right-hand side of the window. Note that the file being downloaded (in this case **wzbeta32.exe**) is a self-extracting compressed file having the .EXE extension.

Once the downloading of the file has started, you are informed of progress by the following window:

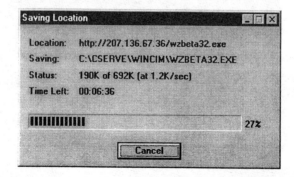

When the downloading of the file is complete, exit the Internet and start up the Windows Explorer. In this case the downloaded .EXE file has been placed in the location C:\CSERVE\WINCIM\WZBETA32.EXE

As this is a self-extracting file, the software can be installed to your hard disc by double clicking on its icon in Explorer.

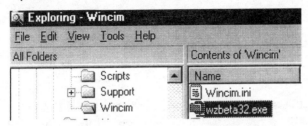

You are then given the chance to specify the folder into which WinZip is to be installed.

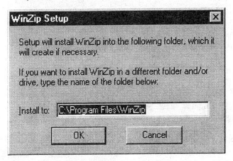

The setting up of WinZip is now complete and the program can be run as a menu option in the usual way from **Start**, **Programs** and **WinZip**.

Downloading Microsoft Internet Explorer 4

Downloading software from the Internet is reliable and convenient, although it can be very time-consuming. At the time of writing, it is possible to obtain Microsoft Internet Explorer 4 as a download, while only version 3 is currently available on CD.

I recently obtained a free copy of The Microsoft Internet Explorer 4 software from the Internet by logging on to the Microsoft Web site, at:

http:/www.microsoft.com/

Then the software was downloaded, before running the resulting .EXE to extract the files. Finally the setup program was used to install the Internet Explorer application in its executable form. However, you must be prepared to tie up your computer and telephone line for a long time (especially if, like me, you are using a modem rather than a fast ISDN line). My download consisted of nearly 16 MB and took over 4 hours!

If you don't want the inconvenience of downloading, you'll have to settle for whatever is the currently released version of the software on CD.

The Shareware Site

This site allows you to download very large quantities of software from easy to use links and menus without needing to know the URLs (HTTP://WWW.........etc !)

As mentioned previously, shareware allows you to download free copies of software - usually of a very high quality. Typically, shareware operates on a "Try before you buy" basis; you can use the software freely for a limited period of say, 20 to 30 days. Usage of the software is monitored and the days remaining and ordering details are usually provided on the opening screen. Once the initial trial period is over you must buy a registered version to continue to use the program.

The Shareware Web site is located at:

http://www.shareware.com

From this site it is easy to download a wide range of software by clicking on the appropriate links:

A weekly chart of the most popular downloads is provided, in this case showing that WinZip was the piece of software most people downloaded. (Downloading a copy of WinZip is described earlier in this chapter).

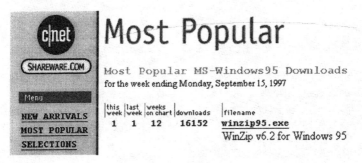

Paint Shop Pro 4

This is a powerful graphics program downloadable from the Shareware site. In particular it can handle 30 graphics formats including the .GIF and .JPG/JPEG formats used for Internet graphics. So Paintshop Pro is a useful tool for viewing and manipulating pictures downloaded from the Internet.

To download a copy of Paint Shop Pro 4 from the Shareware site, simply enter its name in the search box. Clicking on the resulting link **psp32.zip** starts the download process. Paint Shop Pro is a substantial package, requiring nearly half an hour for the download as shown in the **Saving Location** box below.

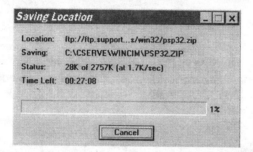

Note in the above box, that the file is being downloaded from a location starting with the letters **ftp**. These letters refer to the server which holds the shareware we are downloading. FTP servers are used specifically for downloading and uploading files. The name FTP is an acronym for File Transfer Protocol - a protocol being a set of rules, in this case for transferring files between computers. It is possible to access the FTP servers directly if you know the URL; this topic is discussed in more detail in the next chapter.

The above **Saving Location** box also shows that the Paint Shop Pro file being downloaded, **psp32.zip,** is a compressed file since it has the .ZIP extension.

So before the software can be installed on your hard disc and run from the **Program** menu it will need to be extracted. This can be done using a program like WinZip or PKZIP for Windows (as discussed later in this book both are available off the Internet).

Extracting Paint Shop Pro

As I was using CompuServe while downloading Paint Shop Pro, the .ZIP file was placed in the directory C:\CSERVE\WINCIM. This can be seen in the Windows Explorer.

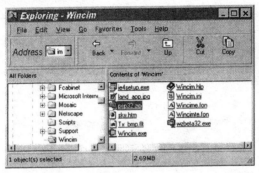

There are options under **File** to extract this file to a specified location or to convert it to a self-extracting .EXE file. However, if you have a copy of WinZip installed, clicking on **psp32.zip** in Explorer will start up WinZip. The file is then extracted by WinZip in a series of simple stages which only require the user to click on

Next a few times. Then you have the option to **Install Now** which installs the software and adds **Paint Shop Pro** to the **Program** menu. When you run the program the window, shown right, appears.

Capturing Internet Text and Graphics

You may wish to look at Internet pages at leisure or have permanent copies of them on paper. One option is to print the page while logged on, using **File** and **Print** from the menu bar in your browser (The Microsoft Internet Explorer or Netscape Navigator, etc). However, printing is a relatively slow process and can result in computer "crashes". Therefore it is usually more efficient and cheaper to download the Web page to your hard disc. Then disconnect from the Internet and carry out any viewing or printing off-line.

As an example, I recently needed to obtain some information on antique pianos. Entering "antique piano" into the Yahoo! search engine quickly led to the site of a specialist piano dealer - Besbrode Pianos of Leeds.

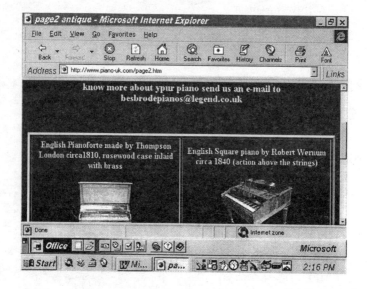

The previous screenshot was captured by pressing the **Prt Sc** key while on-line using Microsoft Internet Explorer 4. This placed the screen image onto the clipboard. Then it was pasted into Word. Alternatively it could be pasted into Microsoft Paint where it could be cropped or modified then saved in the popular Windows bitmap format having extension .BMP. This bitmap file could be used as a piece of clip art and imported into various Windows applications like Word.

Saving a Web Page to the Hard Disc

Alternatively, you can put a copy of the Web page onto your hard disc by selecting **File** and **Save As...** while you are on-line to the Internet. Then you specify the directory into which the pages should be stored. This will be stored as a special Internet file with the .HTML (HyperText Markup Language) extension. To view it later (off-line) you will need to double click on its icon. Your browser such as Internet Explorer or Netscape Navigator should start up (off-line) with the Web page in the window. Unfortunately this method only saves the *text* from the Web site onto the hard disc. The pictures are left out, as shown below.

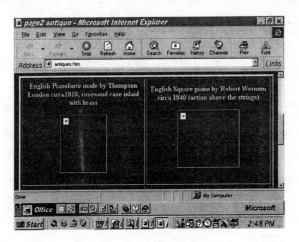

Saving Internet Graphics

Pictures can be captured while on-line to the Internet
by clicking the right mouse button over the required
picture on the Web page. From the resulting menu, the
Save Picture As... option allows you to place the
image in a folder of your choice.

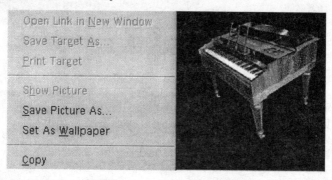

Internet Explorer 4 allows you to save these pictures in
either the bitmap (.BMP) or .GIF format. Internet
pictures are often saved in either the .JPEG
photographic format or as .GIF (Graphics Image
Format) files. They may be viewed off-line by double
clicking on their icon in the Windows Explorer. The
browser should start up, with the picture in its window.

If your browser doesn't have
an image viewer you can
download a copy of LView
Pro from the Internet, using
the method described earlier
for WinZip. The Web site for
LView Pro is:

http://www.lview.com/

CompuServe subscribers have a built in program, **ImageView**, accessible from **Start**, **Programs** and **CompuServe**.

Downloaded images may be converted to Windows bitmap format in an image viewer and imported into Microsoft Paint and altered or manipulated.

The History Folder

Microsoft Internet Explorer uses a folder (**Windows\History**) to keep the links or shortcuts to the most recent Web pages visited. You can use this off-line by double clicking on the URL (the line starting with **http://www...** after the icon) in the Windows Explorer to view and print both text and graphics.

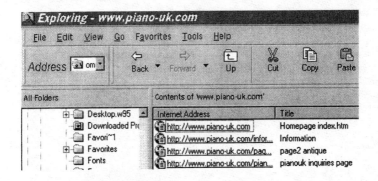

When you are on-line to the Internet you can select **History** from the Explorer 4 menu bar and the contents of the **History** folder appear in their own window:

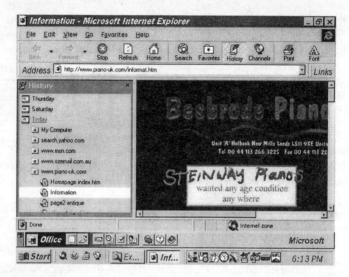

Selecting any of the locations in the left hand window takes you straight to that Web page as shown above. This is useful if you don't know the URL of a Web site you wish to return to after a recent visit. By default Internet Explorer 4 saves the locations for the last 20 days' surfing. You can alter the number of days for which site locations are kept using the box shown below, accessed in Internet Explorer from **View** and **Options**. You can also remove the **History** files by selecting the **Clear History** button.

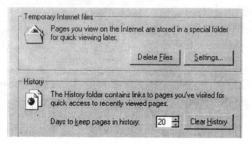

A Cache of Temporary Files

When you first visit a Web site it can take a long time for the pages to be downloaded from the Internet on to the screen, especially if they are heavily laden with graphics.

Subsequent visits to the site should see the pages appear much more rapidly. This is because copies of the Web pages are stored on your own hard disc the first time you access the site. In future visits the pages only have to be retrieved from your hard disc, not from the server hard disc probably hundreds of miles away. This temporary store on the hard disc is called a cache. In this context the cache is really just another folder, although you can also have caches in the memory. In Internet Explorer the location of the cache is:

C:\Windows \Temporary Internet Files

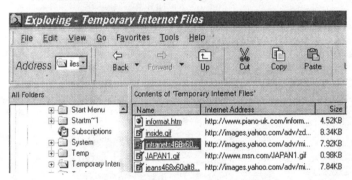

You can view the Web pages off-line by clicking on the appropriate line on the right hand side of the Explorer Window.

Details of the folder **Temporary Internet Files** are displayed by highlighting the folder in Windows Explorer, then selecting **File** and **Properties**.

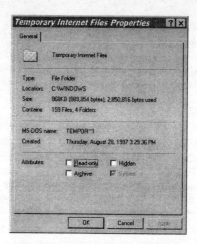

The **Delete Files** option shown below should be used regularly to save hard disc space. This option can be accessed using **View** and **Options**.

You can adjust the amount of hard disc space allocated to **Temporary Internet Files** in Internet Explorer 4 by selecting **View**, **Options** and **Settings** as shown in the following dialogue box.

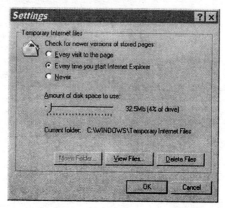

By default, the hard disc represented above has 32.5 MB reserved for the temporary files, but this can be altered by moving the sliding pointer. As shown in the previous dialogue box, there are options to check whether the Web pages in the cache on the hard disc should be replaced by newer versions if they are updated on the Internet.

Netscape uses a folder **Netscape\Cache** to store its Internet temporary files as shown below.

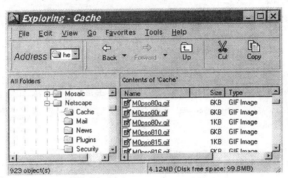

The **Preferences** box allows Netscape users to adjust the size of the available **Disk Cache** and to get rid of old Web pages using **Clear Disk Cache Now**. This box is selected from **Options** and **Network Preferences**.

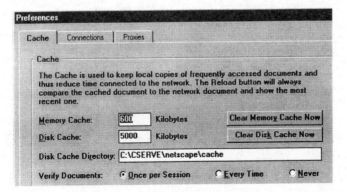

The Favorites Folder

This is a method of simplifying access to the sites you wish to visit regularly by placing the names of the sites in a menu. This is obviously much more convenient than remembering and typing in a URL such as HTTP://www.awesomepages.com/.

The name of the site is placed in the **Favorites** (that's how it's spelt on the screen) folder and can be accessed from either **Start** and **Programs** or from the **Internet Explorer** menu bar.

The user simply adds the sites they wish to visit regularly to the **Favorites** folder. These can be organised into a hierarchy of folders and sub-folders just like the folders as discussed earlier in the off-line Windows Explorer.

As an example, we will add a menu item to take us directly to the site of the Isle of Man Hang Gliding Club at http://www.york.ac.uk/~socs66/manx/.

With the required Web page running on line, click the right button over the page. A menu appears from which **Add to Favorites** is selected.

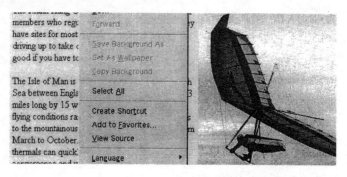

You are then given the opportunity to enter a name for the site as it will appear on the menu. At the same time you can select the folder into which the name is to appear or create a new folder if necessary.

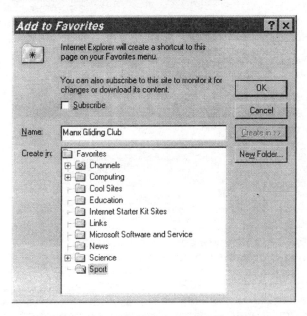

In this example I created a new folder called **Sport** into which was placed the currently active Web page, renamed as the menu item **Manx Hang Gliding** .

You can then access this Web page from either **Start** and **Favorites** or by selecting the **Favorites** folder from the menu bar across the top of the Internet Explorer screen as shown below.

This presents a choice of folders containing easily accessible sites as shown below. Clicking on **Manx Hang Gliding** takes you straight to the site. This is obviously quicker and easier than typing in the URLs.

Organising Favorites

Management of the **Favorites** folder and its sub folders is carried out using the **Organize Favorites** option selected off the Internet Explorer menu bar as shown.

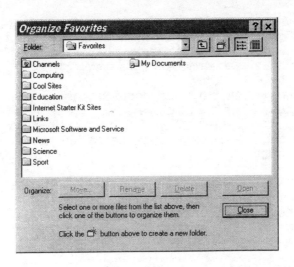

The **Organize Favorites** option provides the main facilities necessary to manage folders and sub folders, such as to create new folders in a hierarchical structure and to **Move**, **Rename** and **Delete** folders and **Favorites**. This work can be carried out off-line to save connection charges.

Summary: Capturing Internet Files

- Whenever you go on-line to the Internet, your computer automatically saves files containing text and graphics from the sites visited. These are placed in a temporary folder or "cache" on your hard disc. These cache files should be deleted regularly to save disc space.

- Many Web sites provide links which allow you to download high quality software. This may be entirely free or request payment after an evaluation period.

- Major companies such as Microsoft and Netscape allow copies of some of their latest software to be downloaded free of charge. "Beta" copies or "pre-release" test versions are also available.

- Many utility programs needed in the handling of Internet files are also available. These include file compression/extraction programs such as WinZip and software for viewing different Internet graphics formats.

- The text and graphics from Internet Web pages can be downloaded and saved locally on your hard disc. These may be viewed off-line in your Internet browser or in a program such as LView Pro or Paintshop Pro. (Both downloadable).

- Internet Explorer maintains a **History** folder of the most recent sites visited. These can then be accessed directly through menus created by the system rather than typing in the URL for the site.

- A similar system of menus is used to access sites which the user has placed in the **Favorites** folder. These sites can be arranged in a hierarchy of folders created by the user.

- All files downloaded from the Internet should be carefully checked for viruses as described later in this book.

3. FILE TRANSFER USING FTP

Introduction

FTP (File Transfer Protocol) is the key to the treasure chest of thousands of files held on the Internet. FTP is a program which enables all sorts of files (text, graphics, sound, software, etc.) to be transferred between computers across the globe. Mostly this means downloading files to your computer from a remote **FTP Server** computer; **uploading** files (including Web pages) from your hard disc to the server is also possible.

In the previous chapter we looked at the way well-known software packages could be obtained by simply clicking on a download link on the appropriate Web site. This is fine for the popular packages which have been set up to be accessed in this way. The FTP servers, however, contain thousands of files ranging from books, academic reports, and technical information to complete fully featured programs.

The principle of FTP is that you log on to your normal Internet provider - like CompuServe, Microsoft Network, etc. Then you log on to the remote FTP server containing a huge library of files. Unless you have a special account with the FTP server, you log on with the user name **Anonymous** and your e-mail address as the password. Once on-line to the FTP server you can move around the public directories, selecting files to download to your hard disc. (Directories are areas where files are stored; Windows 95 uses folders instead).

You may also upload (i.e. send) large program files, for subsequent downloading by a friend or colleague. (Small files may be sent as attachments to e-mail messages as discussed in the next chapter)

Accessing FTP from CompuServe

CompuServe makes access to the FTP servers relatively simple. From the CompuServe Main Menu select the **Go** button, then type **ftp** in the **Service** box.

Then you can either choose to look at a menu of popular FTP sites or access a specific site.

The popular FTP sites can easily be selected from the menu below.

If you wish to look at other sites, you will need to type in the **Site Name**, as shown in the **Access a Specific Site** window below.

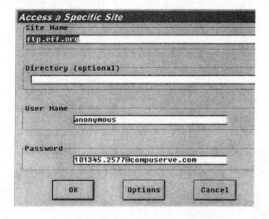

In this example, CompuServe has filled in the **User Name** and **Password** automatically. Clicking **OK** should lead you to the FTP server, where you can move about the directories as if you are in the Windows Explorer. Then you select the public directory **/pub** from which you can download files.

You may also be able to upload files from you hard disc to the selected directory on the FTP server.

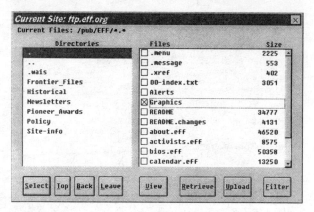

Usually there is a README file which can be opened by clicking **View**. This should give useful information about the site. You should also be able to view an index text file describing the files in the directory. To download a file from the FTP server to your own hard disc, select the required file in the right hand panel of the **Current Site** box then click **Retrieve**. By default the file is downloaded into the CompuServe folder **Cserve\Download** but you have the option to specify a different folder.

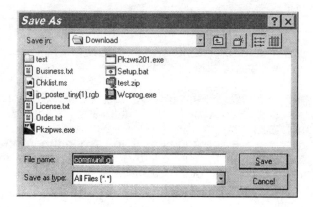

Progress of the download is indicated by the **Retrieve File Progress** window.

Certain types of Internet file, such as those in the .GIF graphics format, will need to be opened in a suitable viewer such as Paintshop Pro, LView Pro or Netscape Navigator working off-line. The Internet Explorer 4 can also open .GIF files and convert them to .BMP files. This makes them compatible with popular programs like Windows 95 Paint. (As discussed in the next section.)

Uploading Files

You can transfer files from your computer to a directory on an FTP server to which you have access. Select the **Upload** button as shown on the **Current Site** window shown earlier in this section. Then from the resulting upload window shown below, browse through your hard disc to find the file to be uploaded.

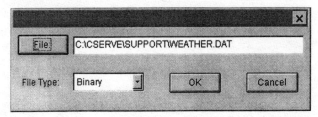

51

The **File Type Binary** should be selected. This is suitable for the transmission of all types of file including text and graphics.

Accessing FTP from an Internet Browser

If you know the location of the FTP server, you can log on to it by entering the URL in your Internet browser. For example the URL for the Electronic Frontier Foundation site is:

ftp://ftp.eff.org

Using Internet Explorer 4, the URL is entered as shown:

In this example I have moved into the graphics sub-directory of the public directory i.e. **/pub/graphics**.

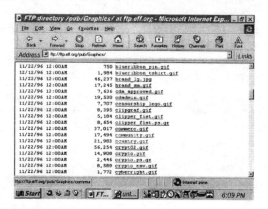

Clicking the file **index.html** displays a description of each file in the directory. To download a particular file in the current directory, click on its name. In this case I selected a graphics file, **community.gif**.

The file is downloaded onto your hard disc into the directory (or folder) **Windows\Temporary Internet Files.** This folder also contains a lot of temporary files placed there by Windows during its normal operation.

The downloaded graphics file, **community.gif** may be viewed later by running Internet Explorer 4 off-line.

Internet Explorer 4 allows you to save the file as a .BMP file in a folder of your choice. (Then the downloaded .GIF file can be deleted from the folder **Windows\Temporary Internet Files** to save hard disc space).

Once saved as a .BMP file the graphic can be loaded into a program like Paint and edited if necessary.

Summary: File Transfer Using FTP

- FTP is the main method of transferring files across the Internet. The files may be very large and represent different types of data - books, reports, graphics, sound and programs.

- FTP servers, or sites, often have public areas available without subscription. The user logs on with the name Anonymous, using their e-mail address as the password.

- If you know the URL of the FTP site (e.g. **ftp://ftp.eff.org**) you type it into your browser like a normal Web URL. CompuServe provides a system of menus leading to popular FTP sites.

- The user moves about the directory structure of the FTP server until the required file is found. Clicking on the file starts the download process. The downloaded file may be saved in a temporary folder on the user's hard disc or in a specified folder.

- If the file is compressed (but not a self-extracting .EXE file) it will need to be extracted using a program like WinZip. If the file is a computer program, after extraction it will need to be installed or set up like any new piece of software.

- The public may *upload* files to some FTP servers so that other people can download them. Please note, however, that for small files (under 500 Kilobytes) it may be simpler to send them as an attachment to an e-mail message. (Please see the next chapter).

- **N.B.** As with all files imported onto your hard disc, files downloaded from the Internet should be thoroughly checked for viruses, as described later in this book.

4. MANAGING YOUR E-MAIL

The e-mail messages you send and receive can be organised as files in a hierarchy of folders on your hard disc. Although many messages may be no more than a few lines of text, these can accumulate and use up precious hard disc space. In addition, various types and sizes of files may be sent and received as **attachments** to e-mail messages.

So it's a good idea to prune the system of unwanted e-mails. Those you want to keep can be categorised and archived in specially created folders.

The e-mail program Microsoft Exchange is an integral part of Windows 95. When Exchange is invoked from **Start** and **Programs** you are presented with a screen quite similar to the Windows Explorer.

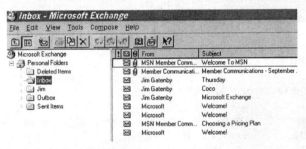

Initially you are presented with the **Inbox** folder containing incoming mail, as shown above.

The data in the columns along the right-hand panel, **From**, **Subject**, **Received** and **Size** may be sorted into order by clicking on the column title. Unread mail items are highlighted in bold text. Those with a paper clip next to the envelope icon have an **attachment** - a file which has been "clipped" to the e-mail and sent with it. The windows for the other folders, **Outbox**, **Deleted Items** and **Sent Items** operate in a similar fashion.

Microsoft Exchange is a tool dedicated to the sending and reading of e-mail, but it also has some similar facilities to Microsoft Windows Explorer, with a **File** menu and "drag and drop" operation for moving files and folders. New folders can be created and manipulated to provide a hierarchical structure. Messages are saved as files and these can be deleted or archived by moving to a different folder.

The four folders **Deleted Items**, **Inbox**, **Outbox** and **Sent Items** are integral components of Exchange and cannot be deleted. However, you can create your own additional folders if you want to organise your messages into different categories.

Most of the work to manage the Exchange folders can be carried out off-line to save connection charges; only the actual sending and receiving operations require you to be on-line.

When you enter a new message in Exchange and click on the **Send** icon, the message is immediately placed in the **Outbox**. Unsent messages remain in this folder until the next time you go on-line in Microsoft Exchange. The messages are then moved to the **Sent Items** folder. The **Outbox** folder is emptied automatically by the system, but the **Sent Items** folder will grow to unmanageable levels unless it is pruned regularly. (You can switch off the option to **Save a copy of the item in the Sent Items folder** using **Tools**, **Options** and **Send**)

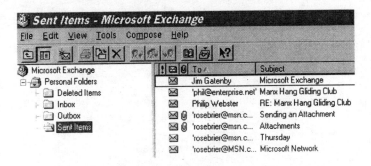

Unwanted items can be removed from any of the folders by selecting the item and pressing the **Delete** key or using **File** and **Delete** from the menus.

When you delete an item from the **Inbox**, **Outbox** or **Sent Items** folders in Exchange it is moved to the **Deleted Items** folder. However, to remove items permanently from the hard disc, you must then remove them from the **Deleted Items** folder. A warning appears to make sure this is what you really want to do.

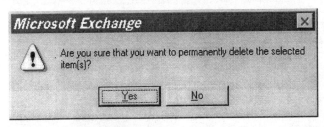

Alternatively you can switch on the option to **Empty the 'Deleted Items' folder on exiting** using **Tools**, **Options** and the **General** tab as shown in the **Options** box.

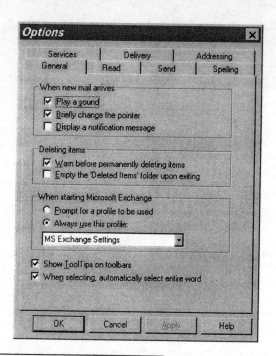

Creating Your Own Mail Folders

If you send or receive a lot of mail which you want to keep for future reference, you'll need to organise it into separate folders. Suppose, for example, you communicate socially with friends, receive business messages relating to work, and handle mail in your capacity as secretary of a Sub-Aqua club. We might therefore wish to create folders called, for example, **Social**, **Business** and **Sub-Aqua**.

To create a new folder, first select **Personal Folders**, then **File** and **New Folder.** Now type the name of the new folder in the resulting window.

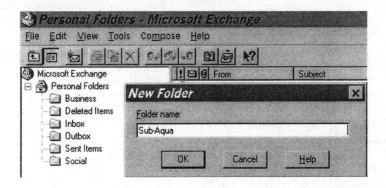

You can then create a hierarchy of sub-folders within the newly created folders, as shown for the Sub-Aqua club:

The **File** menu in Microsoft Exchange has the options to **Move**, **Copy**, **Delete** and **Rename** files and folders. (Apart from the four permanent Exchange folders mentioned earlier.)

Now it's a simple task to drag the mail items from the **Inbox** (for example) and drop them into the new folder that you have created for them. This **moves** the file from its original location.

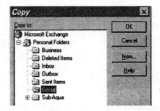

You can also use the **File** menu in Exchange to **Copy** and **Move** files.

E-mail Attachments

When you send an e-mail message, you can include with it an additional file as an attachment. The file might, for example, be a wordprocessing document, a spreadsheet, graphics or sound file. When the file is received, the attachment appears as an icon adjacent to the message. When the icon is double clicked, the attached file is opened, running in its associated program. So, for example, an attached spreadsheet file might open up in Microsoft Excel or similar, when you double click its icon on the e-mail page.

Attachments can also take the form of a shortcut to a Web site. When you double click on the icon, the Web site is accessed. This type of attachment is used in the **Welcome To MSN** e-mail shown below.

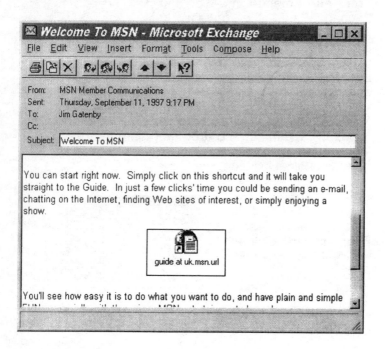

Sending an Attachment

As an example, I will send an e-mail to myself, with a spreadsheet file as an attachment. First the e-mail message is entered in the normal way. Then you select **Insert** and **File** from the menu bar, as shown below.

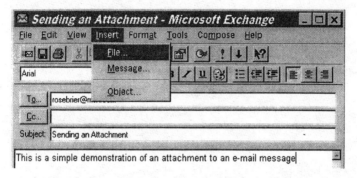

The **Insert File** box opens to allow you to select, from within the hierarchy of folders on your hard disc, the file which is to be attached to the e-mail. If the file is not simply plain text, **Insert as...An Attachment** should be switched on.

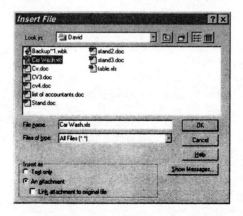

Clicking **OK** inserts an icon for the attachment into the message. When the message is received into an **Inbox**, the presence of the attachment is denoted by a paper clip on the left of the message details.

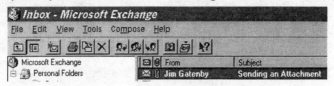

Opening up the message shows the icon for the attachment below the text of the message.

In this example the attachment is a small spreadsheet file. Double clicking on the icon opens up the attachment, running in its associated program, in this case Microsoft Excel.

The attached file can be saved separately on the hard disc, in a directory of your choice, by selecting the icon for the attachment then using **File** and **Save As...** from the menu bar. Make sure **Save these Attachments only:** is switched on. Enter the **File name:** for the attachment and select the folder into which it is to be placed. Clicking the **Save** button will save the attachment file separate from the e-mail message which delivered it.

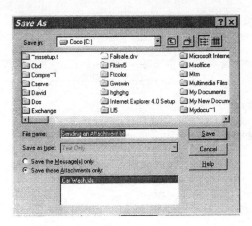

Receiving Attachments

The sending of different types of file as attachments has been made possible by the development of a protocol or standard called **MIME** - Multipurpose Internet Mail Extension. In order to accept the attachments you send, the receiving computer must also be using an e-mail package which is compatible with the MIME standard.

Compared with the transmission of simple e-mail messages consisting only of plain text, the sending of different types of attached file puts extra demands on the system. This is because the more complex spreadsheet, wordprocessing, graphics, and sound files must be translated into the code used for transmitting e-mail text.

The use of attachments is therefore only suitable for relatively small files - otherwise the process is too slow. FTP, as discussed earlier, should be used for the transmission of really large files (above about 500 Kilobytes).

Summary: Managing Your E-mail

- Copies of e-mail messages are automatically saved as files in folders on your hard disc.

- Unwanted messages should be deleted regularly to save disc space and to prevent the accumulation of unwieldy lists of mail items

- Programs like Microsoft Exchange allow e-mail to be organised as files in a hierarchy of folders. New folders can be created and managed using similar facilities to those provided in the Windows Explorer.

- Many types of file (text, graphics, sound, spreadsheets, etc.) can be "clipped" to an e-mail message and sent as an attachment.

- Attachments received with an e-mail message can be saved as separate entities in a specified folder on your hard disc.

- E-mail programs which use the MIME protocol are necessary for the sending and receiving of e-mail attachments.

- All e-mail files should be carefully checked for viruses, as described later in this book.

5. BACKING UP THE HARD DISC

The Hard Disc (Drive) is the main medium for keeping permanent copies of your work; it corresponds to the filing cabinet in the traditional office. In order to put the hard disc in context we must first be clear about its role in the operation of the computer.

Many new computer users are confused by the term "memory". When the computer gives an "out of memory..." error, some users mistakenly believe their hard disc is full. In fact, this error refers to the microchips which form the computer's memory.

Types of Storage

There are two main ways of storing data:

1. Temporary storage in the computer's memory.

2. Permanent storage by recording on a magnetic medium such as the hard disc (and also floppy discs, tape and ZIP discs)

The Memory

The memory (also known as RAM - Random Access Memory) consists of several banks of microchips, known as SIMMs.

The memory is a temporary store for the programs and data which are currently being used. Any data which is typed in the computer will sit in the memory until:

- You switch the computer off

or:

- The data is overwritten by new data which you have typed in or loaded from disc.

65

Saving Your Work

The memory is said to be volatile i.e. its contents are lost when the power is removed. In order to keep a permanent copy of the data it should be saved on a hard disc or 3.5 inch diskette.

Permanent Storage - The Hard Disc Drive

The hard disc (drive) is a sealed unit built inside of the computer and physically inaccessible unless you remove the computer's metal casing. The magnetic disc surfaces (platters) on which programs and data are recorded are an integral part of the drive unit which also contains the moving heads used for reading and writing data.

The hard disc is usually designated as the C: drive, and consists of a set of metal discs coated in a magnetic material and rotating about a central spindle. The hard disc unit is housed in a metal case and is sealed to prevent particles of dust from entering and damaging the disc surfaces, which are machined to very fine tolerances.

In normal use the hard disc rotates at several thousand revolutions per minute, making it a very high performance device but also vulnerable to catastrophic failures. If the moving head which "reads" the data from the disc touches one of the disc surfaces (resulting in a "head crash"), the disc surface will be scratched and some, if not all, of the data will be lost. (A head crash might, for example, be caused by moving or bumping the computer while the hard disc is running.)

The 3.5 inch "Floppy" Diskette

The internal hard disc drive described above is not to be confused with the 3.5 inch floppy disc or diskette. Some people mistakenly think that the 3.5 inch disc, because of its rigid plastic case, is actually a "hard" disc. In fact, the magnetic disc material (known as the "cookie") inside the plastic case of the 3.5 inch disc is really quite flexible and "floppy", just like the original 5.25 inch floppy disc.

The 3.5 inch diskette is portable and very easily inserted into or removed from the floppy disc drive (FDD). In the past, most new software packages were supplied on floppy disc. Now, with the increasing size of new packages, this role is steadily being taken over by the CD-ROM. (A large package such as Microsoft Office requires over twenty 3.5 inch discs, but can comfortably fit onto one CD.) Transferring data from a single CD is obviously much faster and less prone to errors than from a large number of 3.5 inch diskettes.

However, the 3.5 inch disc is still a very cheap and convenient way of transferring a few files or a small piece of software from one computer to another.

The Contents of the Hard Disc Drive

The hard disc in the computer system is equivalent to a filing cabinet in the traditional office. Permanently saved on the magnetic surfaces of the hard disc are most of the programs and data essential for the running of your computer. The hard disc is not to be confused with the memory or RAM of the computer, which is the temporary store used to hold programs and data while they are in current use. When you switch the computer off the contents of the RAM are cleared, but the contents of the hard disc remain in place.

The hard disc normally contains:

- The systems software such as the Windows 95 operating system needed to start and run the computer.

- The applications software such as your word-processor, database, DTP, graphics or games.

- The work you have produced and saved as files - the wordprocessing documents and spreadsheets, etc.

The internal hard disc is generally a well-designed component which can perform reliably for many thousands of hours over several years. However, due to possible accidents and natural disasters, it is by no means uncommon for individuals and even companies to "lose" the entire contents of a hard disc.

In some cases the files of data may still reside on the disc after a disaster, but the user loses the ability to retrieve them by normal methods. (There are companies who specialise in the recovery of data from damaged hard discs but this is an expensive process).

With a hard disc drive you really have got "all of your eggs in one basket" - if it fails without adequate backup arrangements, your computer will be useless. The software stored on your hard disc may well be worth thousands of pounds and the data files may represent hundreds of hours of work. Therefore the loss of this electronic filing cabinet may represent a personal catastrophe or spell financial disaster for a small business.

Although, fortunately, head crashes are fairly unusual, there are many other ways in which the contents of the hard disc may be lost or damaged.

Ways to Lose Your Data

- The computer or some of its internal components such as the hard disc may be stolen.

- You may accidentally delete important files by giving the wrong command.

- Someone may deliberately wipe or format the entire disc.

- The data on the hard disc may be corrupted by a software error or an electrical failure like a power cut.

- The data may be damaged by one of the many computer viruses which can attack your system from various sources.

- The hard disc may be damaged by the spilling of drinks or the data corrupted by exposure to a magnetic field by placing it near to another electrical device such as a stereo speaker.

- The computer itself may be totally wrecked by events such as fire, flood, earthquake or explosion.

- After several years' faithful service, the hard disc may reach the end of its useful life.

Although some of these disasters are unavoidable, their effects can be reduced if you have backup copies of all important files.

Your Exposure to Risk

You can assess your exposure to risk by considering the following factors:

- How long would it take to completely restore your system in the event of a total hard disc failure?

- Could you re-install all of the essential software ? (Can you quickly find all of the installation discs and CDs ?)

- Does the hard disc hold essential business files - customer records, accounts or CAD files etc?

- Have you have spent months typing in your magnum opus, perhaps a dissertation or a new novel ?

- What about your Curriculum Vitae, which has been honed and polished over the years, into the masterpiece it is today. The day your CV gets wiped is likely to be the moment when you want to apply for a new job, and time will be critical.

- Who else uses the computer - might they damage files ? (Does the business computer on which your livelihood depends also double up as the family games machine ?)

- Does anyone import "dodgy" files from diskette or the Internet which might spread viruses and wipe the hard disc?

The Backup Process

The only way to reduce the risk of a computing catastrophe is to make duplicate or backup copies of all important files (both software and data files).

A backup is a copy of some or all of the files from a hard disc drive onto another "non-volatile" storage medium, such as a diskette or tape. (Non-volatile means the data is permanently saved after the computer is switched off - unlike data in the memory, which is cleared when the power is removed.)

The purpose of a full backup is to allow a computer system and much of its software and data files, to be completely restored in the event of a total disaster, including the loss of the computer itself.

For important files, the backup discs or cartridges should be kept in a safe and secure place, away from heat and magnetic fields and preferably in a separate building away from the computer. This also applies to the original installation discs and CD-ROMs from which software may need to be re-installed.

Although it is convenient to make backup copies onto another part of the same hard disc, these are of little use if the hard disc is damaged or the computer is stolen. Making backups on the same hard disc only gives protection against the deletion of some of the files.

For important work, a planned backup strategy is essential, with a system of several discs or tapes used in rotation. For a small backup consisting of a few important files, one or more floppy discs may be adequate to store the data. Alternatively, a full backup will copy the entire contents of the hard disc onto a special high capacity magnetic tape cartridge.

Capacities of Magnetic Storage Media

In order to appreciate the type of backup storage medium required, it is necessary to be familiar with some of the jargon relating to the representation of data and the units used to measure storage capacities. Then you can estimate the amount of space required to backup a particular set of files.

The basic unit of computer storage is the byte. This is the amount of space taken up by one character when it is temporarily stored in the computer's memory or permanently saved on a disc or tape cartridge. A character is typically a letter of the alphabet (both upper and lower case), a punctuation mark or keyboard symbol, or a digit or number in the range 0-9.

Every character is represented in the computer by a code made up of eight binary digits. The binary code employs only the digits 0 and 1 and is used because it is relatively simple for an electronic device like a computer to represent two states.

Examples of character codes used are as follows:

Character	Binary Code
A	0 1 0 0 0 0 0 1
a	1 1 1 0 0 0 0 1
9	0 0 1 1 1 0 0 1

The fact that computers perform their internal work using the binary system based on the number 2, rather than our normal decimal system based on 10, gives rise to some rather strange units for large numbers of bytes. The most common units used for describing computer capacities are the kilobyte, the megabyte and the gigabyte.

> **1 kilobyte (K)** is approximately 1000 bytes (1024 to be exact)
>
> **1 megabyte (MB**) is approximately 1000K or about a million bytes (1,048,576 to be exact)
>
> **1 gigabyte** (**GB)** is approximately 1000 megabytes.

A kilobyte represents about a third of a page of text on A4 paper. One megabyte is very roughly the text in a novel of about 300 pages. If you include pictures and scanned images amongst the text, the amount of storage space required increases alarmingly. At the time of writing, files saved on disc or tape are usually stated in kilobytes and the memory or RAM is given in Megabytes. Hard disc capacity is quoted in either megabytes or (increasingly) in gigabytes.

Comparing storage capacities

Medium	Typical Storage Capacity
3.5 inch Floppy Diskette	1.44MB (uncompressed)
Hard Disc Drive	500 - 3000MB (3GB)
Tape Cartridge	400MB - 8GB
CD-ROM	660MB
ZIP / Jaz Drive Discs	100MB - 1GB

Choice of Backup Medium

From the above figures it can be seen that in order to backup an entire hard disc, a tape system is needed. It would simply be too big a job with today's large hard drives to back up onto numerous 3.5 inch diskettes. You might consider installing a second hard drive, but this would not be a very secure system since it would not cover the situation where the computer was stolen or damaged by fire.

The disadvantage with the full tape backup is that it is slow, often taking 2 or 3 hours to back up a large hard drive. For this reason, the full tape backup is normally scheduled to take place during the night.

The 3.5 inch diskette is still a very quick and convenient backup medium for copying selected files occupying up to about 10 megabytes. The backup software should allow the backup to span several discs and request additional blank "floppies" as they are needed.

File Compression

The backup software normally includes an option to compress the files as they are being saved to the backup medium. This can effectively double or even treble the effective storage capacity. So a nominally 1.44 megabyte diskette can hold more than 3.0 megabytes of compressed data and a 400 megabyte tape cartridge can hold about 700 megabytes of user files. (Not all of the 400 MB is available to the user).

Removable Hard Discs

These have the capacity of a small hard disc drive combined with the portability of a floppy disc. Two of the most popular systems are the Iomega Zip and Jaz drives. The Zip drive takes removable discs of 100MB capacity while the Jaz discs can accommodate up to 1 GB.

I have been using an Iomega Zip drive for about a year and have found it to be extremely reliable and useful. While not having the capacity to replace the tape cartridge for a full system backup of a large hard disc, the Zip drive nevertheless has many valuable functions. It is many times faster than a tape drive and is therefore ideal for quick backups of software and data files which are too large for floppy discs.

The text and screenshots for this book amount to nearly 30 MB but fit easily on to one Zip disc. For extra security I have a couple of Zip discs each with a complete copy of the manuscript. To achieve the same peace of mind with floppy discs would require about 42 discs and an impossible amount of disc management.

With your important work copied onto Zip discs and the software safe on CD ROM (or Zip disc), you can quickly recover from a hard disc disaster.

Although the Zip drive can be managed with the normal Windows 95 tools, there is also a set of Zip Tools which provide additional features. These include **Iomega Copy Machine** which allows a removable disc  to be duplicated by swapping discs in a single drive. Alternatively, you can use the **Two Drive Copy** to copy between any two discs on the system.

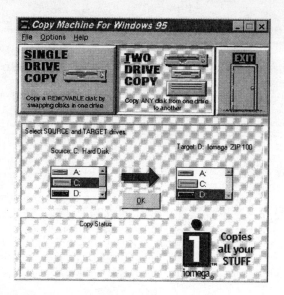

The removable hard disc drive is however, very much more than a backup device. Once installed on your system it can be used just like any other hard disc drive. Files can be moved to and from the removable drive by dragging and dropping in My Computer or Windows Explorer.

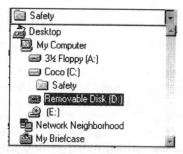

In applications like Word you simply select drive D: (or whatever) to save your work on the Zip drive.

The external version of the Iomega Zip drive is particularly handy for transferring large files and software to other computers. You just plug the Zip drive's cable into the printer port on the other machine and install the driver. On a machine with one fixed hard disc drive and a CD-ROM drive, the Zip drive becomes drive D: while the CD-ROM is drive E:

Summary: Backing up the Hard Disc

- The contents of your hard disc, including both software and data files, represents a huge investment of time and money, probably exceeding the value of the computer itself.

- The main reason for backing up files is to enable a recovery of the contents of your hard disc, which are vulnerable to damage or loss.

- Without an adequate backup system, loss of the hard disc contents can be a catastrophe, because of the time and costs involved in restoring the software and data files.

- A secondary reason for backups is to transfer files between computers; for example, between work and home.

- Archiving is the copying of files which are seldom used, onto a disc or tape, in order to save hard disc space. The archived files can be retrieved later, if necessary.

- Full system backups copy the entire contents of the hard disc onto a tape cartridge. The tape has a storage capacity equivalent to several hundred floppy discs.

- In a partial backup, small selections of files can be backed up onto floppy discs.

- A modified or incremental backup copies only those files which have changed since the last backup.

- File compression (discussed later) can greatly increase the storage capacity of disc or tape.

- Backup discs and tapes should be stored in a secure place well away from the room where the computer is located.

- Removable Hard Discs, such as the Zip and Jaz discs, can perform a valuable role as a fast backup medium for large groups of data files and software. The Iomega Zip drive has its own powerful tools to facilitate the copying of files and discs.

- The external Zip drive is portable and can easily be connected to other computers for the transfer of data files and software. The system is much faster and has far greater capacity than the floppy disc.

- The Removable Hard Disc can also operate as an efficient extension to the fixed hard disc system, using normal Windows 95 features, such as My Computer and the Windows Explorer, for managing files.

The backup process introduced in this section is discussed in more detail in the next two chapters.

6. FEATURES OF BACKUP SOFTWARE

The copying of files and directories can be carried out using "drag and drop" in the Windows Explorer as described previously. This is quite efficient for copying small sets of files and directories to "floppy" discs on an occasional basis. However, for systematic, regular backups, dedicated backup software is available which automates the process and provides a lot of additional facilities.

Windows 95 includes Microsoft Backup free within the original set of floppies or CD, but this may still need to be installed on your particular system. If you buy a tape drive unit, such as HP Colorado, dedicated backup software will be included with it.

Some of the features of dedicated backup software are:

• Full backups of an entire drive.

• Selection sets of files which are backed up on a regular basis.

• Scheduling of backups at regular times outside of working hours.

• Backup to disc or tape storage.

• Error checking to ensure the backup is accurate.

• File compression to maximise storage space.

• Incremental backups which only backup files that have changed (since the last backup).

• Restoration to the original location or a specified location on the hard disc.

File compression software, such as WinZip and PKZIP for Windows, is particularly useful for backing up selected files rather than the full backup carried out using a tape system. File compression maximises the available space on the backup storage medium, which is often one or more "floppies", but could equally be the same or another hard disc. File compression is described later in this book.

Microsoft Backup

Microsoft Backup may already be sitting on your system and ready for use. If not, you can still use it and it's free - it just takes a little time to set up. If you've still got your Windows 95 CD or installation discs, then you most certainly already have a copy of Microsoft Backup. However, it may not have been "ticked" for inclusion when Windows 95 was originally installed on your hard disc. Microsoft Backup is a complete backup program and is actually a version of HP Colorado Backup, supplied with the very popular HP Colorado tape drives. The software is compatible with a number of tape drives. If you haven't got a tape drive in your machine, you can still use the software to backup onto floppies.

Finding out if Microsoft Backup is Installed

If MS Backup has already been installed on your system, you will find it in the **System Tools** window, accessed via **Start**, **Programs** and **Accessories**.

If **Backup** doesn't appear in the **System Tools** window, then it will need to be installed from the original Windows 95 installation discs or CD as shown in the next section.

Installing Microsoft Backup

From the Windows 95 startup screen, select **My Computer** and **Control Panel**.

The Control Panel window should appear as shown below.

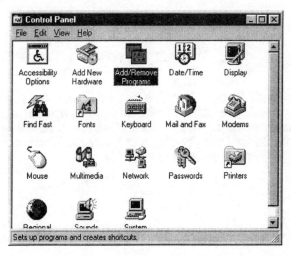

Now select **Add/Remove Programs** and from this
window select the **Windows Setup** tab. As shown
below, this will reveal the Windows 95 components
which are already installed.

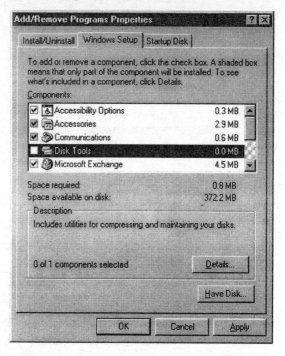

Microsoft Backup resides within **Disk Tools**, so click
the box on the left. (The tick should appear against a
clear background). Click **Details** to reveal the
contents of **Disk Tools** and make sure the square to
the left of **Backup** is ticked.

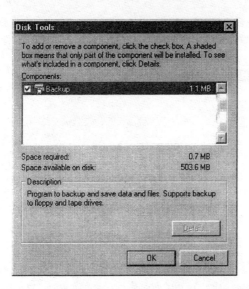

Click **OK** to exit **Disk Tools** . You will be asked to place your Windows 95 CD or diskette in the drive.

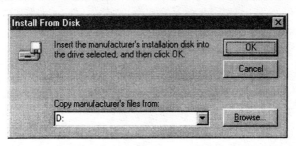

Now click **OK** and Microsoft Backup will be installed on the main **Programs** menu.

To launch **Backup**, select **Start**, **Programs**, **Accessories**, **System Tools** and **Backup**.

Spanning Floppy Discs

Suppose you want to back up a group of files contained in a folder. For example, I have recently started a new project and have completed the Introduction and the first 3 chapters. These are all saved on the hard disc in a folder called "New Project" within my personal folder named "Jim".

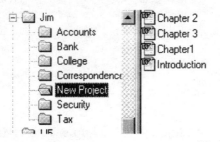

One solution might be simply to place a blank disc in the A: drive then "drag" and "drop" the folder "New Project" onto the icon for the A: drive, using the Windows Explorer.

Unfortunately this does not work, with the following message appearing on the screen:

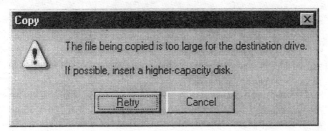

The problem is that the folder "New Project" and its 4 files occupy 4 megabytes of the hard disc, as indicated at the bottom of the Windows Explorer screen. The 3.5 inch floppy we are attempting to copy onto can normally hold only 1.44 megabytes of data.

However, we could accomplish the task quite easily using Microsoft Backup because of two important features:

- There is an option in Microsoft Backup to compress the files on the backup media. So, for example, a floppy disc can be made to hold up to 5MB instead of the usual 1.44MB.

- If necessary, the user is requested to enter another floppy disc, so the backup can span several discs.

Floppy versus Tape

It would have been possible to back up the folder and its 4 files to a tape. However, for a small partial backup like this, "floppies" are much faster. It is also more convenient if you want to transfer the files between computers, since the tape would require both machines to be fitted with compatible tape drives. The tape backup is essential however, for large backups and full backups of an entire hard disc, when the task of changing large numbers of floppies becomes totally impractical. (Several hundred floppies would be needed.)

Using Microsoft Backup

The software must be capable of 3 main functions in order to provide a complete recovery from disaster:

1. Backup the required files to separate floppy disc(s) or tape.

2. Compare the backup files with the original files on the hard disc - to ensure the backup was accurate.

3. Restore the backup files to the hard disc. Restoration involves copying the backup files back to the original locations on the hard disc. Or, in the case of theft or fire etc., the backup files would need to be restored to an entirely different computer.

Launching Microsoft Backup

The program is started as mentioned previously, from **Start**, **Run**, **Programs**, **Accessories**, **System Tools** and **Backup**. First ensure that the **Backup** tab is selected. Then select the folders and/or files you wish to back up.

In this case, because I want to back up all of the files in the folder "New Project", the box to the left of it is clicked and a tick appears against a clear background. (The box to the left of "Jim" is ticked against a grey background, indicating that not all of the folders in "Jim" are to be backed up.)

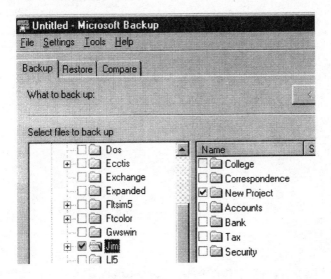

If you open the folder "New Project", which is ticked against a clear background, you will see that all of the files are themselves ticked and therefore included in the backup. Individual files can be included or excluded from the backup by clicking in their box.

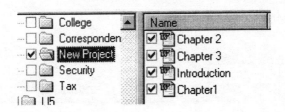

Having selected with a tick the files to be backed up,
we select **Next Step** to specify the destination of the
backup, in this case the 3.5 inch floppy, Drive A:.

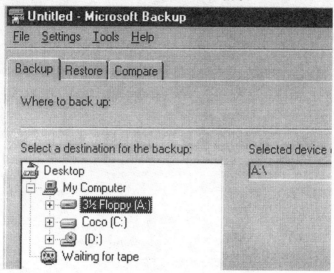

We are now ready to proceed by selecting **Start
Backup** and are given the opportunity to enter a name
for the backup set of files. You can also enter a
password to restrict access to this particular set of
backup files.

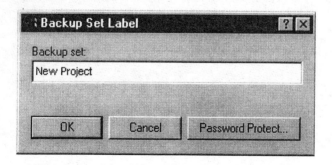

Windows 95 allows the use of long filenames so it is possible to make the name of the backup set fairly meaningful - especially helpful if you are looking through your discs for a backup in several months' time. The backup set is saved as a special type of file (having the QIC filename extension). Therefore if the file is subsequently retrieved or restored from the backup disc, Microsoft Backup will need to be used (discussed later). Applications like Microsoft Word cannot read backup files.

Next click OK to start the backup. A window appears to tell you how the backup is progressing.

In this case, the compression option allowed over 4Mb to fit onto one 1.44Mb (nominal) floppy disc. Otherwise the program would have requested another floppy to be inserted.

Comparing Backup Files with the Originals

The **Compare** process can be run from the tab in the main **Backup** window. However it is probably more convenient to set this to run automatically at the end of every backup. This is done by selecting the **Backup** tab and ticking the **Verify** box in **Advanced options**. The **Compare** process checks the accuracy of the backup compared with the original files. The results of using **Compare** on the backup described above are as follows:

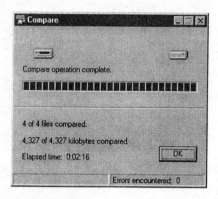

The Backup Options

Microsoft Backup allows you to specify how the backup is to be carried out. This includes the opportunity to do an incremental backup - only backing up files that have changed since the last backup. Other important options include the ability to switch compression on and off and to specify an automatic compare/verify operation at the end of the backup. Another option allows you to erase tapes and discs before backing up - otherwise the backup will be added to what is already there.

The backup options are accessed from the main
Microsoft Backup window via **Settings**, **Options** and
the **Backup** tab.

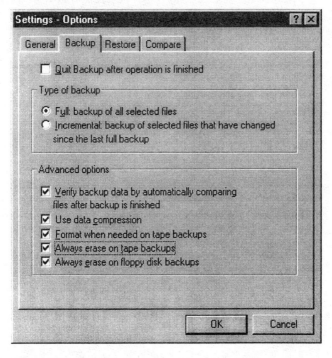

Keeping the Backups Safe

At this point, your backup should now be safely stored
on one or more floppy discs. These should be clearly
labelled and locked away in a different physical
location from your computer, to guard against the risk
of fire, theft or some other disaster such as flooding. If
you've used meaningful names for your backups it will
be easier to identify them at a later date.

The Restoration Process

Restoration is the process of copying files from the backup disc or tape, back onto the original hard disc or onto a completely different hard disc. The entire backup set of files may be restored or, alternatively, it is possible to restore just a small selection of files.

Although we hope backups will never need to be restored in a crisis, it makes sense to find out how to do the job beforehand. Microsoft Backup has a set of **Restore** settings which provide various options to control the restoration process.

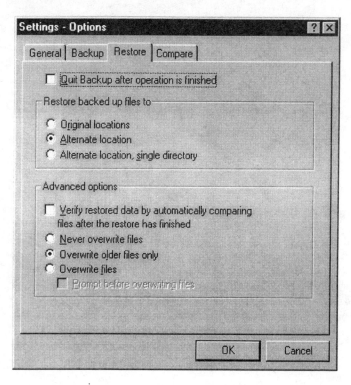

With the **Original locations** button selected, the backup will return to where it came from when it was first saved on the hard disc. With **Alternate location** selected you will be asked to specify a folder into which the backup is to be restored. (Obviously you must use this option if you were restoring to another computer). If you need a new location for your backups, create a folder using the Windows Explorer. For this example, the backup will be restored into a folder I have created called "Home for lost backups".

If you have the **Overwrite older files only** button switched on, you will not be able to restore files to their original location on the same day as the backup, since the original files are not regarded as older. However, switching the **Overwrite files** button on permits this.

Restoring the Backup

Start Microsoft Backup as described previously and select the **Restore** tab. Now select **3½ Floppy(A:)** as the location to restore from. Click on **Next Step** and enter the password for this particular backup set.

Now select the folders/and or files which you wish to restore. This is done by clicking in the boxes to the left of the files you wish to restore.

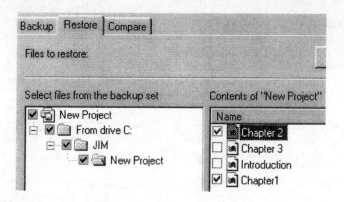

In the example above, I have only selected two of the four files in the folder "New Project" to be restored. Now select **Start Restore** and because we are not restoring to the original location, we are asked to select the location required. In this example, the location is "Home for lost backups".

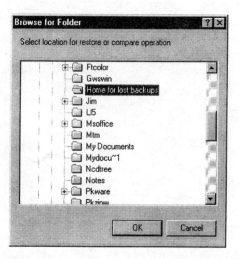

Clicking **OK** will cause the restore to commence and a dialogue box will let you know how it is progressing.

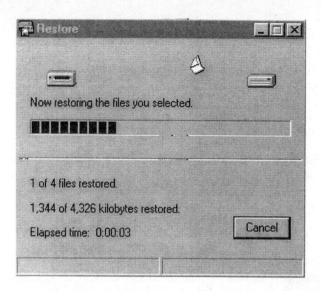

At the end of this process your files will have been restored to their original location or to a folder which you have specified. A dialogue box will appear giving the details of the completed backup.

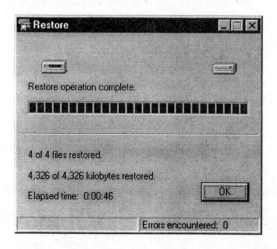

Summary: Features of Backup Software

- Windows 95 already includes dedicated backup software - Microsoft Backup.

- If you buy a tape drive, backup software will be included, such as HP Colorado for Windows 95.

- Backup software allows you to copy to floppy disc, tape cartridge, or removable hard disc (ZIP drive). (Backups to a hard disc within the computer do not provide protection against theft or fire, etc.)

- Floppy discs are suitable for small backups of selected files. A full backup requires a tape system.

- Backup software includes the option to compress the files onto the backup storage medium, more than doubling the capacity.

- Windows 95 allows long filenames; backups can be given meaningful names which help in their identification if needed at a later date.

- The compare or verify option checks that the files on the backup medium are an exact copy of the original files on the hard disc.

- Files can be restored to the original folder or to a specified folder, perhaps on a different hard disc.

- You can restore all of the files from a backup or just a small selection of files from within the backup.

- It's a good idea, after a backup, to do a test restoration of a few sample files, just to check that the backup and restoration system is working correctly.

7. TAPE BACKUP SYSTEMS

Why Use Tape ?

The floppy disc backups discussed in the previous section are suitable for selective backups consisting of no more than a few megabytes of files. Backing up an entire hard disc of one gigabyte or more onto floppies is not viable since hundreds of discs would need to be inserted and replaced in the floppy disc drive. Probably the most cost-effective backup medium at the moment for the home or small business user, for a full backup, is the tape cartridge.

The Travan tape drive technology is becoming a standard, with cartridges classified TR1,TR2,TR3 and TR4 having storage capacities ranging from about 400 MB (800 MB compressed) to 4 GB (8 GB compressed). These are only nominal figures and in practice the space available for your files will be somewhat less. This is because some of the tape will be used by the computer system itself to manage the files; "headers" are added to identify files and "Inter-block gaps" are included to separate groups of records.

It is important to check before buying any tape backup system that it can make a **Full System Backup** of your hard disc onto a single cartridge. The full backup is essential if the entire hard disc fails, or is severely damaged or stolen.

Making a full tape backup is a lengthy process, taking a few hours to copy a large hard disc. Therefore it is usual to set up an automated backup, scheduled to take place outside of working hours, usually overnight. If a single tape cannot accommodate the full backup, the process will be halted in the middle of the night, and the computer will "sit" waiting for another tape to be inserted. As this won't happen until next morning, the backup will then have to be completed during working hours, preventing normal use of the computer. This defeats the object of the automated backup, which should proceed unattended, at a time when the computer is not being used.

Another device sometimes used for backing up is a second hard disc drive. The disadvantage of this is that it provides no protection whatsoever if the computer is stolen or damaged in a fire or flood, etc. Other developments in backup media include removable hard discs (ZIP) drives, writable CD ROM and optical discs.

There is usually a choice of internal or external tape drives. The internal drive obviously provides a neater and more compact solution; the external drive is more portable if you want to transfer a backup to another computer.

Fitting an Internal Tape Drive

You don't need any special tools to fit a tape drive - just a small screwdriver. This really is a task which anyone can do - you don't need any technical or electronic expertise. A brief outline of the installation is as follows:

- Make sure the computer is switched off before touching or working on any components.

- Take the cover off the computer and remove one of the blanking plates covering a vacant "bay" at the front of the machine.

- Slide the tape drive into the vacant bay in the casing and secure at the sides with the 4 small screws which should have been provided with the drive.

- Connect the tape drive to the floppy drive controller using a data cable. (This is a wide, flat, ribbon cable with a red stripe down one edge). You can either use the existing floppy drive data cable or use the new ribbon cable normally provided with the tape drive. Refer to the tape drive installation guide - the position of the red stripe relative to the tape drive is critical.

- There should be at least one spare set of brightly coloured power leads terminating in a white connecting plug. Carefully plug a set of power leads into the back of the tape drive.

- Replace the computer casing and switch on.

If the tape drive subsequently doesn't work, (after you've installed the accompanying software), switch off the computer and remove the casing. Check the position of the coloured stripe on the ribbon cable, relative to the tape drive; try swapping the cable round so that the stripe is in the alternative position. (Remember always to switch off before touching or removing any of the components).

Some packages include a diagnostic program which performs a large number of write operations to test that the system can record properly. Then a corresponding number of read operations check that the data can be retrieved from the tape. If this test is satisfactory, any errors in your subsequent backups are most likely to be in the quality of the original data files which were copied from the hard disc. (Methods of checking and repairing the recording surfaces of the hard disc are covered later in this book).

All operations with tape, such as backing up, comparing and restoring, take very much longer than equivalent disc operations. In fact, they can take a few hours, so it's often more convenient to leave them running overnight.

Installing the Software

When you buy a tape drive, the package should include a disc containing the backup software. Place the disc in the floppy drive and follow the instructions given in the installation guide, for installing the software. (e.g. select **RUN** and enter **A:\setup**). The backup software will then be installed onto your hard disc and can be accessed from **Start** and **Programs** like any other Windows 95 Application.

The following pages give an overview of tape backups using Colorado Backup for Windows 95, the software which is provided with the popular HP Colorado Tape drive. It is virtually identical to Microsoft Backup which was discussed previously. (Microsoft Backup being an integral component of Windows 95). HP Colorado includes all of the features described in the previous section covering Microsoft Backup.

Making a Full System Backup

Preparing a Tape Cartridge

Invoke Colorado Backup from **Start**, **Programs**, **Colorado Backup for Windows 95** and **Colorado Backup** as shown above. Place a tape cartridge in the drive. If the tape is not pre-formatted it will need to be formatted using the **Tools** option in **HP Colorado**.

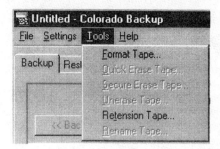

It's obviously worth buying pre-formatted tapes if you can - formatting your own tape is an operation which can take a few hours. Also on the **Tools** menu above is the **Retension Tape** option. This only takes a few minutes and should be carried out regularly - before every full backup if possible.

The Full System Backup is essential if you are to recover from a major disaster to your hard disc. This backup includes not only your important data files representing hours of toil, but also the program files or applications, such as Microsoft Office. Also included in the backup are an important set of files known as the system registry. The registry files are an essential part of the Windows 95 operating system.

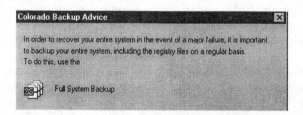

When you install the Colorado software, an icon is created on your desktop to enable you to select the Full System Backup directly. Double clicking on the icon will start the Full System Backup. The Full System Backup can also be started from the Windows 95 **Programs** menus, within **Colorado Backup for Windows 95**.

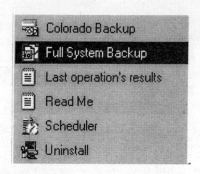

Scheduled Backups

Making a Full System Backup is a lengthy process and can take the computer out of normal use for several hours. Therefore it may be more convenient to schedule the backup to take place outside of working hours - the middle of the night is a popular time. Obviously the machine must be left running, with a tape cartridge in the drive and preferably with all other applications shut down. Colorado Backup for Windows 95 has an **Automated Daily Backup** already set up. All you need to do is set the time and switch **On** in the dialogue box.

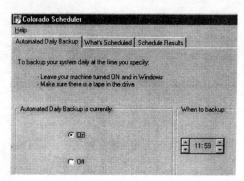

The backup can also be set to take place at specified times on certain days of the week.

Selecting the Files to be Backed Up

As mentioned previously, it is possible to back up a selection of files or folders by clicking on the box to the left of the file or folder.

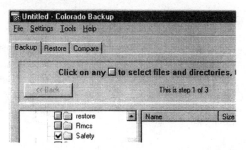

After you have selected the files and folders to back up, clicking **Next** will move you on to the dialogue box which allows you to specify the destination for the backup. In this case the destination is the Colorado Tape Drive.

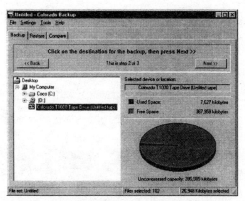

Clicking on **Next** allows you to set the options for the backup, including the use of data compression and automatic verification. You can also give a name to the backup and add a password, to stop anyone else from accessing the files on the backup tape.

File Sets

Anyone sharing a computer on a regular basis might well organise their work into personal folders, so that their files are not mixed up with the work of other people. In this situation you would probably wish to make regular separate backups of your own files and folders. The solution to this is to create a **file set** by selecting the required group of files and folders. Even if you do not share a computer, you may still need to back up just a selection of files or folders. The file set becomes a permanent separate entity, which can be backed up more easily than selecting the files every time a backup is made.

Creating a File Set

You set up the backup in the normal way, selecting the files and folders to be backed up, then select the destination for the backup and set the backup options. Then the selection is saved as a file set through the **File** and **Save As...** menus. The file set is actually saved in the **Backup** folder within the **Windows** folder. Whenever you want to back up this set of files in the future, you simply start the **Windows Explorer** and double click on the name of the file set.

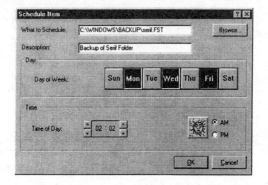

Backing Up Only Modified Files

Each time you do a full system backup, a large number of files will be copied to tape, even if they haven't changed since the last backup. This is wasteful of time and computer resources. There is an option within the backup software which allows you to copy only those files which have changed since the last backup. These are known as modified backups. Detecting changed files is made possible by a property or attribute in every file, known as the archive bit.

The archive bit is a "flag" which indicates whether a file has changed since the last backup. If you make an alteration to one of your Word files, say, the archive bit will be "set" when the file is saved on the hard disc. When you next specify a modified backup, this file will be backed up to tape because it has been flagged as having been modified. During the backup process, the archive bit on the copy of the file on the hard disc is cleared to indicate that it has been backed up to tape.

If you don't subsequently change the file in any way, the next time you do a modified backup, this file will not be copied to tape. Modified backups should only be used as part of a complete backup strategy which must also include regular full system backups.

Restoring Files from Tape to Hard Disc

The method of restoring backup files from a tape cartridge is basically the same as described in the previous section covering restoration from floppy discs.   However, since tape drives are relatively slow devices (and also hold very much more data), restoration of a large backup from tape can take several hours.

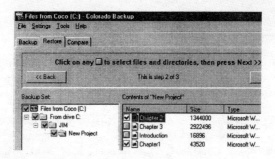

As with restoration from floppy disc, it is possible to restore an entire backup or just a selection of folders or files from within the backup tape. It is also possible for the destination of the restored files to be their original location on the hard disc, i.e. the files are restored to the same folder in which they were originally created.

Alternatively it is possible to restore files to an entirely new folder, perhaps on a different hard disc drive.

Recovering from a Complete Hard Disc Failure

If you are unlucky, the whole of your hard disc may be corrupted or wiped. Or, if your hard disc has suffered a mechanical failure such as a head crash, a new hard disc drive may need to be fitted. Alternatively in the worst case, your whole machine may have to be replaced because of a disaster such as fire or theft.

As long as you have at least one recent full system backup, and any subsequent modified backups, (stored in a very secure separate location) you should be able to recover your data completely.

The value of your data (a best selling novel perhaps?) can far exceed the cost of a new computer system.

A suggested recovery procedure is as follows:

1. If necessary "boot" the machine from a floppy system disc and format the hard disc.

2. Install Windows 95 from the original CD or the "floppy" installation discs.

3. Re-install your backup software, such as Colorado Backup for Windows 95, from the installation discs.

4. Start the backup program and restore your most recent full system backup to your hard drive. The option to overwrite files should be selected.

5. Restore any modified backups in the order in which they were created.

Developing a Backup Strategy

Even with a tape backup system capable of copying the entire contents of the hard disc, it is still possible for disaster to strike unless a reliable backup strategy is devised. Below are some possible scenarios which could lead to a crisis; they can be avoided with a little planning.

• You only have a single tape and you overwrite it with each new backup. There is a problem during the backup, causing the data on both the hard disc and the tape to be corrupted.

> **Your data is lost for ever and the files must be re-created from scratch**

- You only back up once a week and the hard disc fails just before the backup is due.

   A whole week's work will be lost.

- You do an automated daily full system backup with a separate tape for each day, but there is a serious problem (possibly caused by a virus) which goes undetected for over a week.

   All of the backup tapes would be damaged.

The ideal solution is to have a lot of backup tapes covering as long a time span as possible. However, backup tapes are expensive and the time to manage the backup process must also be considered.

A simple but expensive solution would be to have a separate backup tape for each day and to set a daily automatic backup. Then to have two or three similar weekly sets of tapes, to be used in rotation. This would help to overcome most of the problems listed above.

Or you could use fewer tapes by backing up only modified files on certain days. These should fit onto one tape. A possible backup strategy would then be:

1. Dedicate one tape to an automated weekly full system backup. Use another tape for the remaining days of the week to hold all of the daily modified backups.

2. Repeat the process the following week, but using two different tapes.

3. Complete a three week cycle with a third pair of tapes.

4. In the fourth week, return to the first set of tapes and overwrite them. Continue to rotate the tapes in a three week cycle.

Summary: Tape Backup Systems

- A tape backup system which can store the entire contents of your hard disc on a single tape is necessary for unattended backups.

- Fitting a tape drive is not a daunting task, even for the non-technical person.

- Tape backup systems allow the automatic scheduling of backups at specified times (often overnight) and on particular days. Full system backups of the entire hard disc can take several hours.

- The creation of file sets automates the scheduling of backups of frequently-used groups of files.

- Applications such as Microsoft Word, Excel, Access, etc, should be shut down before a backup is run. Otherwise files left open in running applications may cause problems during the backup process.

- A full system backup (on an additional tape) should be made immediately after new software and hardware have been installed.

- A backup strategy is needed which provides several separate backup sets of tapes - then if one backup tape is corrupted others will still be available.

- An economical strategy combines full system backups with a series of modified backups.

- Backup tapes should be clearly labelled and stored in a secure place, where there is no risk of fire, flood, theft or corruption from magnetic fields.

- The original installation CDs and floppy discs for all your software should be kept safe - especially Windows 95 and the backup program itself. The latter will certainly be needed if a complete restoration is called for.

- Tapes and tape drives should be maintained according to the manufacturer's instructions. This includes re-tensioning the tape regularly.

- The hard disc should be checked for errors by the regular use of Windows 95 ScanDisc, as discussed later in this book.

- Frequent virus checks should be carried out with an up-to-date package such as Norton AntiVirus or Dr. Solomon's Anti-Virus Toolkit, discussed later.

8. HARD DISC CARE

Introduction

Hard disc drives are incredibly reliable for mechanical devices which rotate at several thousand rpm. Out of more than 200 machines with which I am familiar, only one or two hard disc units have been replaced in the last two years. However, the integrity of *data* stored on the magnetic surfaces of hard discs is a different matter. Apart from the risk of viruses (covered in detail in a separate chapter), the efficiency of the hard disc can be impaired by a number of factors.

Constantly deleting files and saving new ones causes the hard disc to become *fragmented*. Any remaining space may be scattered, requiring extra travel by the read/write heads which save and retrieve files.

Virtual Memory

When Windows 95 is working away on memory hungry applications, it uses part of the hard disc to supplement the memory or RAM chips (SIMMs). This "virtual memory" takes the form of a Temporary Swap File on the hard disc. The size of the swap file increases and decreases automatically according to the demands of the applications being run, within the limitation of the available free disc space.

You can look at the virtual memory of your computer by selecting **Start, Settings**, **Control Panel** then clicking on the **System** icon. System

The **Performance** tab opens up the following **System Properties** window.

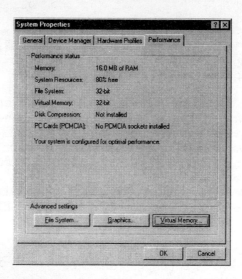

From the **System Properties** window shown above, select **Virtual Memory**.

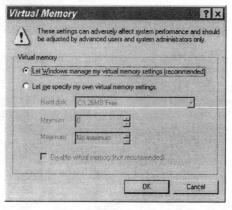

The Virtual Memory dialogue box above allows you to specify the size of the swap file or to allow Windows 95 to manage it for you. It is strongly recommended that you allow Windows 95 to determine the size of the virtual memory. Without sufficient virtual memory your computer may run very slowly or even crash.

It can be seen that the size of the virtual memory is limited to the available hard disc space. Clearly machines which are short on memory in the form of RAM chips will need to rely more heavily on virtual memory. This will be indicated by frequent flashing of the hard disc light. In this situation, as data needs to be moved in and out of the swap file regularly, any fragmentation will further impair the performance of the computer.

Defragmenting the hard disc and therefore the swap file, together with maximising the disc free space are therefore essential to the efficient running of your computer.

To organise the available free space into one contiguous or sequential block, Windows 95 provides **Disk Defragmenter**. This is launched from **Start Programs**, **Accessories** and **System Tools.**

Routine Maintenance Tasks

Files may be corrupted if the machine is not shut down properly. This means closing all running applications and their associated files before switching off. Corrupt files may be repaired using **ScanDisk** in **Accessories**, **System Tools** as shown in the above menu box.

Temporary files are created by Windows during normal operation and in theory these should be removed automatically if Windows 95 is shut down correctly. However, in reality, you may well find a large number of temporary files still residing on your hard disc. These should be deleted regularly to save disc space and improve efficiency.

Although the price of hard discs has fallen in recent years, so that capacities of several gigabytes are now quite common, it still makes sense to delete any redundant software and data files. This can best be carried out in Windows Explorer or My Computer. Obviously great care should be taken to avoid deleting files which are still needed. The **Recycle Bin** gives a chance to recover deleted files before they are lost forever. In any case, backup copies of important files should be made before starting any serious delete operations. (Please see the separate chapters on backing up hard discs and files).

Three important maintenance tasks for improving the efficiency of your hard disc are therefore:

- Correct errors in files and disc surfaces using ScanDisk

- Consolidate files and free disc space using Disk Defragmenter

- Delete temporary and redundant files

These methods are discussed later in this chapter.

Hard Disc Properties

You can view the properties of your hard disc by highlighting the C: (or D: or whatever) drive in **My Computer** and selecting **File** and **Properties**. It can be seen from the following report that this particular hard disc is nearly full and some serious deletion of redundant files is called for.

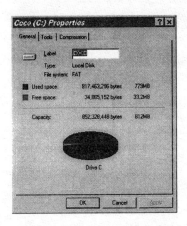

The **Properties** box with the **Tools** tab selected (shown
on the next page) indicates that the hard disc has been
neglected for a few weeks and may benefit from error
checking using **ScanDisk** and compacting using **Disk
Defragmenter**. It is often recommended that these
important housekeeping tasks should be carried out on
a weekly basis (combined with a suitable backup
strategy). Microsoft Plus! is an accessory to Windows
95, which, amongst other things, enables automatic
scheduling of **ScanDisk** and **Disk Defragmenter**.

Using ScanDisk

Scandisk can be started from **Start**, **Programs**,
Accessories and **System Tools**. Or you can use My
Computer to select your C: drive then use **File** and
Properties and **Tools** as shown on the next page.

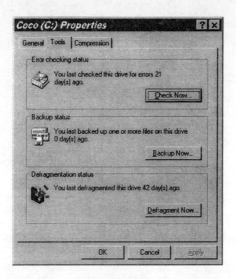

Error checking with **ScanDisk** is started by clicking **Check Now**. This brings up the ScanDisk dialogue box which allows you to choose either the **Standard** or **Thorough** test. The standard test checks only the *files* on the disc drive while the thorough test, which takes much longer (roughly half an hour), also checks for defects on the disc *surface*. There are options to select which disc to scan, including floppies and multiple hard discs, and to fix errors automatically.

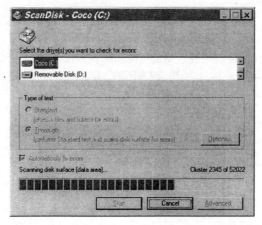

It is recommended that all other applications and any screen saver are disabled while ScanDisk is operating, since open files cannot be checked for errors.

Progress of the scan is indicated as shown previously. When the scan is complete, detailed results are presented as shown in the following **ScanDisk Results** box. In this example, errors were found and corrected by ScanDisk. The results box in Scan Disk is optional and may be switched off in **Advanced**, **Display Summary**.

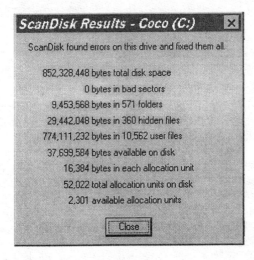

The following **Options** dialogue box in ScanDisk (Thorough Test only) allows the user to prescribe which areas of the disc are to be scanned and to specify testing of the disc by writing to it.

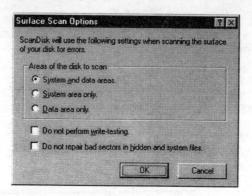

Using Disk Defragmenter

As discussed previously, the purpose of defragmentation is to organise the files and spaces on a disc in order to reduce the time needed for read and write operations.

The program can be started in a similar way to Scandisk from **Start**, **Programs**, **Accessories** and **System Tools**. Or you can use My Computer to select the hard disc drive, C: for example, then use **File**, **Properties** and the **Tools** tab. You are presented with the **Properties** box shown previously, from which you can select **Defragment Now**. This leads to the **Disk Defragmenter** box shown below, which reports on the extent to which the disc is defragmented.

There is an option to select which drives to defragment. These include your hard disc, drive C:, any additional hard drives installed, the floppy disc drive A:, and on my particular machine a Removable Hard Disc or Zip Drive. The **Advanced** button presents the user with an option to perform a full defragmentation of files and free space. Alternatively you can target *files only* or *free space only*.

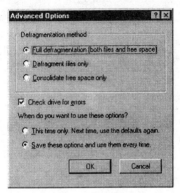

Selecting **Start** invokes the defragmenter and progress is indicated as shown below.

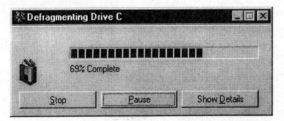

The box on the right is displayed to confirm that the process is complete.

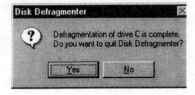

Scheduling ScanDisk and Disk Defragmenter

Regular scans and defragmenting are essential to the efficient running of your computer. So that you don't need to remember this chore, you can automate the task using the scheduler System Agent. This is part of Microsoft Plus!, an accessory to Windows 95.

Once Microsoft Plus! is installed you can find **System Agent** from **Start**, **Programs**, **Accessories** and **System Tools**.

Selecting **System Agent** takes you to the main window which allows you to select which programs are to be scheduled. The maintenance programs ScanDisk and Disk Defragmenter are scheduled to run by default when System Agent is first installed.

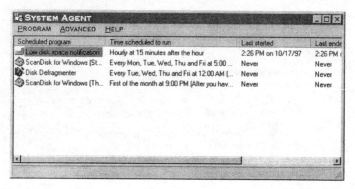

Note that a **Low disk space notification** is also scheduled automatically. By default this is set at 20 MB but the user can alter this figure in System Agent using **Program**, **Change Schedule** and **Settings**. Apart from the disc maintenance programs listed above, it is also possible to schedule other programs.

The settings of time and days of the week can be edited in Systems Agent by clicking on **When To Run**.

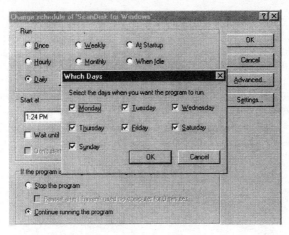

Pruning Redundant Files

Files which are not likely to be needed in future should be removed from your hard disc - although it may be prudent to keep backups on another disc or tape system (as described elsewhere in this book). Redundant files are likely to fall into one of three categories:

- Unwanted and aged data files created by the user - word processing documents, spreadsheets, DTP, etc.

- Temporary files created automatically by the system.

- Software or program files no longer used or replaced by a newer version.

Removing Data Files

Individual files or folders containing files can be removed in Windows Explorer or My Computer. The method is to highlight the file or folder and either select **File** and **Delete** or press the **Delete** key. If a folder is selected the folder and all of the files and sub-folders are deleted. Blocks of files can be selected for deletion by using the left mouse button and the Shift key. If you make a mistake the situation can be retrieved by immediately selecting **Edit** and **Undelete**.

Files and folders deleted in this way are not actually removed from the hard disc, they are merely transferred to a special folder called the Recycle Bin. To permanently remove files and folders you must open the Recycle Bin by clicking on its icon on the desktop. Then remove individual files and folders by highlighting them and using **File** and **Delete**, or pressing the **Delete** key. Alternatively choose the option **Empty Recycle Bin**.

Mistakes can be rectified at this stage using **Edit** and **Undelete**. Files and folders can be retrieved from the Recycle Bin using **File** and **Restore**. This returns the files or folders to their original locations.

Removing Temporary Files

Temporary files are created during normal running of applications such as surfing the Internet; they should be removed by the system when the application is shut down. However, any abnormal end to a process such as a system crash or loss of power supply will result in temporary files remaining as debris on your hard disc.

Temporary files have the extension .TMP and can be found by using **Start, Find**, and **Files or Folders**. To start the search enter ***.TMP** in the **Named** box and click **Find Now**. The list of temporary files should appear as shown below. These may be deleted using **File** and **Delete**. Blocks of files may be selected with the mouse and Shift key.

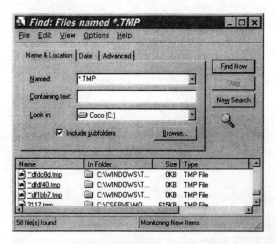

Please Note: All other applications should be shut down before running **Find** since the applications (such as Word) may have temporary files open. Attempting to delete the open files will cause problems.

Removing Software

There may be programs sitting on your hard disc which you never use. Perhaps they've been superseded by a later version. If there's a chance you will need them in future the software should be backed up to a tape cassette or Zip disc, as described elsewhere in this book. Then they can safely be deleted to release hard disc space.

Unfortunately it is not simply a case of deleting the folders bearing the name of the application from My Computer or the Windows Explorer. Programs usually have lots of other files scattered about the system, apart from the files in their main folders. Failure to delete all of the associated files may prevent the system from working or at least display some irritating error messages.

Many programs, such as WinZip for example, have an integral option to uninstall. This is accessed from **Start**, **Programs** then the name of the program.

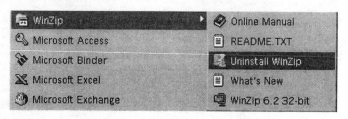

Selecting **Uninstall WinZip** should remove the program and all of its associated files. Before proceeding you are given the chance to abort the uninstall.

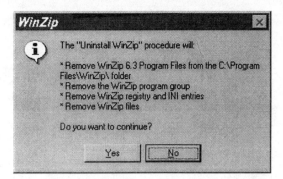

If a program does not have an integral uninstall command, there is an option within Windows 95, accessed via **Start**, **Settings**, **Control Panel** and **Add/Remove Programs**.

Clicking this icon opens up the **Add/Remove Programs Properties** box. With the **Install/Uninstall** tab selected you highlight the program to be deleted then click **Add/Remove**.

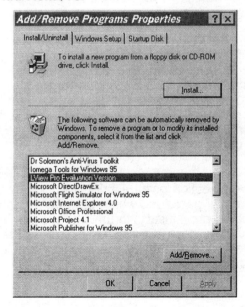

You are then given the opportunity to abort the uninstall operation.

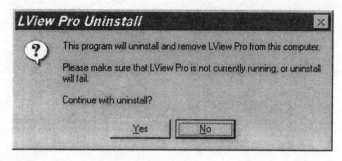

Choosing to continue will remove the program and all of the files associated with it.

The previous pages describe Windows 95's own facilities for maintaining the integrity and efficiency of hard disc drives. Regular use of these features should ensure that your hard disc performs efficiently and reliably.

It must be stressed, however, that all hard disc drives should be backed up to guard against unavoidable disasters such as fire and floods, with the backup tapes or discs stored in a safe and different place. Continual monitoring for viruses with one of the well-known anti-virus packages is also essential. Backup strategies and protection against viruses are discussed in detail in separate chapters in this book.

The next section gives a brief overview of two popular commercial packages which perform much of the work described previously. Norton Utilities for Windows 95 and Quarterdeck CleanSweep both offer additional features for maintaining the integrity and efficiency of hard disc systems.

This is a comprehensive package for monitoring the health of your computer and its hard disc drive. All of the tasks described earlier are covered by various modules within the package and the information is displayed graphically as shown below. **Norton System Doctor** constantly monitors resources such as free disc space and the size of virtual memory. If a problem arises, such as low disc space, the appropriate utility is invoked to rectify the problem.

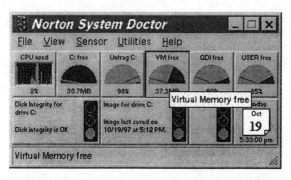

The **Speed Disk** feature in Norton Utilities optimises disc performance by reducing fragmentation of files and compacting free space. The **Space Wizard** identifies files which you may wish to delete and offers suggestions. Possible candidates for deletion would be files which have not been used frequently, temporary files, and surplus Help (.HLP) and graphics files (.BMP) such as those used for Windows wallpaper.

Norton Utilities leads the user through the process of creating a special floppy **Rescue Disk**. This records your original settings so that the computer can be started in the event of a problem with the hard disc. The **Image** feature in Norton Utilities creates a record of vital file information so that files can be recovered and repaired using **Norton Disk Doctor.**

Quarterdeck CleanSweep

CleanSweep has many facilities for maintaining a computer system, but in the context of this chapter its main function is to uninstall programs and remove the resulting debris or "orphaned" files. **Usage Watch** tracks how often a file is opened and **Smart Sweep** monitors the installation of new software. This facilitates any subsequent removal of the software. There is an **Archive Wizard** which uninstalls the software but keeps a compressed version of the program for possible restoration at a later date. **CleanSweep Finders** is a feature which locates redundant files. These may be duplicated, rarely used or "orphan" files - those left behind by main programs which have been removed.

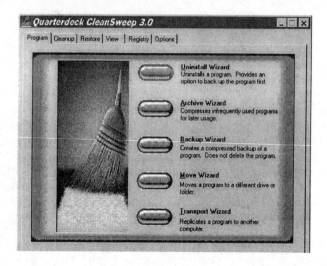

Summary: Hard Disc Care

- Hard disc files become fragmented and cause the system to slow down. Windows 95 Disk Defragmenter re-organises files and compacts the disc free space.

- ScanDisk is a Windows 95 feature which corrects errors in files and on the disc surfaces. Errors may typically be caused by a break in the power supply or a system crash due to a fault in a program.

- Both ScanDisk and Defragmenter should be run regularly (weekly for example) to maintain the integrity of your hard disc. Microsoft Plus! provides System Agent which schedules these programs to run automatically at pre-set times.

- Redundant files and programs should be deleted regularly to maximise free disc space. This can assist the creation of the Temporary Swap File on the hard disc, which acts as Virtual Memory to supplement the actual memory or RAM.

- Files to be considered for deletion include redundant data files like old wordprocessing documents and spreadsheets, etc. Also temporary files remaining on the disc if it has not been shut down correctly. Unnecessary Help files and surplus Windows wallpaper should also be deleted.

- Software which is never used should be either deleted or archived by compressing, to save disc space (using WinZip or PKZIP for Windows).

- Deleting the main folders containing programs does not remove every file relating to the software. Total eradication of all associated files (orphans) requires the use of a special Uninstall facility.

- Software can be uninstalled in Windows 95 using **Start**, **Settings**, **Control Panel** and **Add/Remove Programs**. Some packages contain their own uninstall feature in the list of components in the **Programs** menu.

- Deleted files are automatically sent to the Recycle Bin, which is a folder on the hard disc. Therefore to increase free disc space, the Recycle Bin must itself be emptied.

- Norton Utilities for Windows 95 is a disc maintenance package which monitors a computer system and displays performance statistics graphically. Comprehensive diagnostic, repair and recovery facilities are included.

- Quarterdeck CleanSweep has features for uninstalling software including the removal of orphan files and increasing free disc space by identifying redundant files and making suggestions for deletion.

Please Note:

The above maintenance tasks should be combined with a strategy for regular backing up and virus testing of all discs and files as described elsewhere in this book.

9. FILE AND DISC COMPRESSION

PKZIP for Windows

PKZIP is an example of a file compression program and is a worldwide standard. The software has been around for a number of years in various versions leading to PKZIP for Windows. PKZIP is supplied as Shareware by PKWARE of America and the software alone can be downloaded free of charge from the Internet site at:

http://www.pkware.com/

Alternatively, you can buy the complete package from Atlantic Coast Software of Colyton, Devon. This package includes full documentation and technical support. Several other software packages are available, providing similar file compression functions.

PKZIP might typically be used to:

- Make regular security backups of selected directories and files onto a floppy disc.

- Copy files using compression onto a floppy disc to enable fast and efficient file transfer between computers, e.g. between work and home, or by posting to another user.

- To archive files or complete directories on the hard disc, increasing the amount of free space. You might, for example, compress a piece of software such as a database program which is not used very often but is occupying a large part of the hard disc.

- To send compressed files across a network such as the Internet. Several compressed files are sent as a single packet - much faster and cheaper than sending separate uncompressed files.

The PKZIP software is installed on the hard disc like any other application, and launched from **Start** and **Programs**.

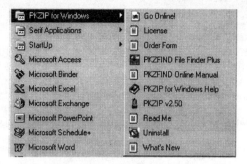

Overview of PKZIP in Action

The main concept is that you create a new .ZIP file which acts rather like a folder. The .ZIP file contains a list of compressed files and is known as an archive file. You then extend the archive file by dragging on to it those files you wish to compress.

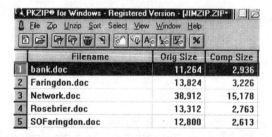

Apart from document files, PKZIP will also compress picture files (.BMP, etc.) and program files (.EXE, etc.) In the above small example, the document files have been compressed to between a third and a fifth of their original size. Some files compress more than others. This is because compression works by picking out common patterns in a file (words like "to" or "the" and spaces, for example) and encoding them in a much shorter binary code than normal. A piece of text will compress more than, say, a complex picture or photograph. So PKZIP allows you to store data on one floppy disc which would otherwise require several. Compressing several files into a single .ZIP file also makes for faster copying and transfer of data.

Before the compressed files can be used again they must be expanded to restore them to their original size. This process is known as unzipping or extraction. Normally, to extract a .ZIP file you must have a copy of the extraction program PKUNZIP installed on your hard disc

However, it is possible to produce a compressed file which can expand itself, without a previously installed copy of PKUNZIP on the hard disc. When the new compressed file is created, instead of being saved as a .ZIP file, it is saved as a special type of .EXE file. This includes, within the compressed file itself, the software necessary to "unzip" itself.

This self-extracting file is therefore accessible on PCs without a separate installation of the PKUNZIP software. As it is an .EXE file, the file can be accessed like any other application, i.e. by clicking on it with the mouse. .ZIP files can be converted to self-extracting .EXE files using a menu option in PKZIP.

The Menu Bar

Although many important tasks can be accomplished by "dragging" and "dropping" and "clicking" with the mouse, PKZIP also has a complete set of menus for all operations. The program runs in its own window with the menu bar across the top and the compressed files in table format underneath.

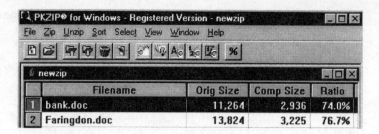

The functions of some the main menu icons are shown below:

Create a new .Zip File

Open an existing .ZIP file

Add files to an existing .ZIP file

Extract files from a .ZIP file

Delete files from a .ZIP file

Test the files before extracting

134

Creating a New Zip File

In the Windows Explorer, select the drive and directory into which you wish to place the new .ZIP file. Now select **New** from the **File** menu. The option to create a new PKZIP file appears alongside the other options for new documents.

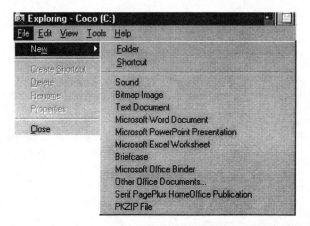

You are then required to enter a name for the .ZIP file. Clicking on this new file name starts up the PKZIP program in its own window, alongside of the Windows Explorer.

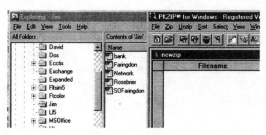

To compress the files you simply drag them from the Explorer and drop them on to the new blank .ZIP file.

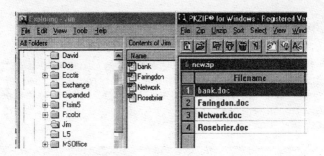

Creating a Self-Extracting File

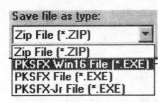

As stated previously, the self-extractor is a compressed file which can be expanded on a machine which doesn't have the PKUNZIP software. First create a .ZIP file as described previously. Then convert the .ZIP file into a self-extracting .EXE file using the **Convert** option in the PKZIP **File** menu. A window appears with various **Save file as type:** options. **PKSFX Win16 File(*.EXE)** is the option for creating a Windows 95 self extracting file.

Extracting ZIP Files

Compressed files must be extracted, i.e. expanded before they can be used in normal applications such as Word and Excel. To expand a .ZIP file, you select the file in its drive and directory in the Windows Explorer. Then you click over the filename or icon with the mouse right button. This brings up a menu which includes the **Extract To...** option.

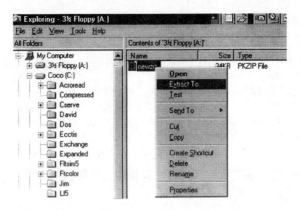

Selecting **Extract To...** opens the Extract window, which allows you to specify the destination directory of your files after they have been expanded.

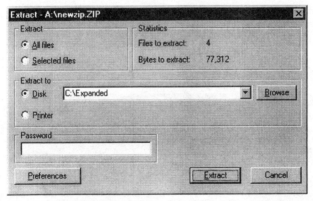

An individual document file in a .ZIP file can also be extracted by double clicking on its row in the .ZIP file table. It is extracted into a TEMP directory for immediate use, to be deleted later. This avoids the risk of overwriting and possibly damaging an earlier copy of the file if it is expanded into its original location with the same file name.

Expanding Self-Extracting Files

These are the compressed files which may be extracted on a computer which does not have PKZIP/UNZIP installed. As mentioned previously, this is possible because the files were saved together with an integral extraction program embedded within them. The self-extracting file has the .EXE extension and appears in the Windows Explorer as an application.

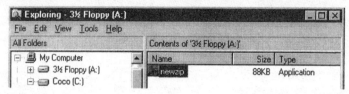

To extract this file, simply double click over the file name or its icon. This launches the extracting program PKSFX in its own window. You now enter the directory into which you want to place the extracted files then select **Extract** to retrieve the files.

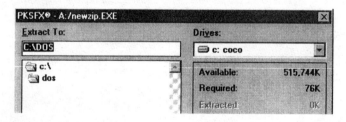

Fine Tuning PKZIP

Like all software packages, PKZIP arrives with a number of standard or default settings prescribed by the manufacturer. The default settings allow the software to function quite adequately, but the user may wish to tailor the settings for their specific needs. This is achieved using the **Zip Preferences** dialogue box accessed from the Zip menu bar.

The preferences are switched on and off using the radio buttons and check boxes. For example the group under **Compression** offers a trade-off between the amount a file is compressed and the speed of the compression operation, e.g. Superfast will provide the least compression.

Attributes are individual properties of each file, such as "hidden" or "read only". Ticking all of these boxes will cause these types of file to be included in the .ZIP file which is about to be created and to take their attributes with them.

The **Archive Bit**, when "set", is an indicator or flag which shows that a file has changed, for example, when text is added to a document file. To save time, you may only want to compress those files that have changed - assuming there is already a full backup in existence somewhere else.

Path Information allows you to specify the precise location on the hard disc (directory, filename, etc.) of the file you are about to compress e.g. **C:\myfiles\bank\overdraft**. This makes it easier to restore the file to its original location, if necessary.

WinZip

This is a file compression program from Nico Mak Computing, Inc. and includes a Wizard feature to simplify the extraction of .ZIP files, such as those downloaded from the Internet.

You can start WinZip from its icon on the Windows 95 Desktop or from the **Start** and **Programs** menu. The user can easily switch between the WinZip Wizard shown below and the WinZip Classic window on the next page.

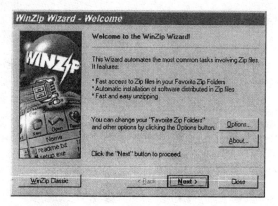

Using the WinZip Wizard, the extraction of software downloaded from the Internet is reduced to little more than a few clicks on the **Next** button. This includes the final installation of the software into a directory of your choice.

WinZip will search your hard drive for folders containing compressed files and arrange them in the **Favorite Zip Folder**, where you can also add or remove folders.

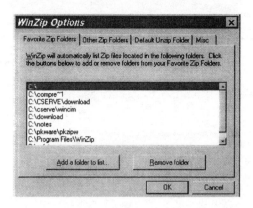

The full range of file compression and extraction activities are provided in WinZip Classic, with the WinZip menu options across the top and the archive of compressed files in a table format underneath.

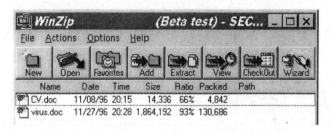

The **CheckOut** feature on the Classic menu bar enables files in an archive to be run from the **Start** menu if they represent programs or viewed if they are documents. If you have a virus checker it can be switched on in CheckOut to examine the archive files.

A free evaluation copy of WinZip can be obtained from the WinZip Internet site:

http //www.winzip.com/

Disc Compression

Programs like PKZIP for Windows and WinZip, described earlier, are designed to compress individual files. It is also possible to compress an entire hard or floppy disc to give 2 or 3 times the nominal capacity.

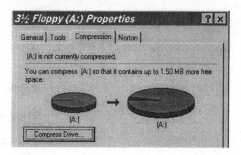

You might well ask why such huge gains aren't exploited by the disc manufacturers in the first place. The answer is that compression will result in some loss of speed in reading and writing files.

Clearly with a very high capacity hard disc drive and the luxury of gigabytes of free space, disc compression is not necessary. However, if your hard disc drive is nearly full it may be worth sacrificing some speed in order to keep using all of your software and data files. The machine I am currently using has a relatively small (by current standards) hard disc drive of 812 megabytes with free space hovering around a miserly 26 megabytes. It's therefore an ideal candidate for disc compression.

Windows 95 is supplied with DriveSpace, it's own disc compression program. A later version, DriveSpace 3, is available to purchasers of the Windows 95 companion Microsoft Plus!

DriveSpace 3

The original Windows 95 compression program DriveSpace can only support compressed drives up to 512 megabytes in size, while the enhanced version, DriveSpace 3, handles a more generous 2 gigabytes. You can check the potential gains from compression using DriveSpace 3 by highlighting the drive in My Computer then using **File**, **Properties** and selecting the **Compression** tab. (Clicking the right mouse button over a disc drive icon also takes you to the **Properties** option).

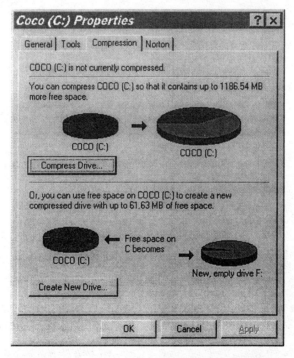

In the case of this particular hard disc, the capacity can effectively be doubled, with an estimated gain of more than 1 gigabyte, using "Standard" compression.

DriveSpace 3 is run from **Start**, **Programs**, **Accessories**, and **System Tools**. It is possible to set different levels of compression, with varying effects on performance, using the dialogue box below, accessed in DriveSpace 3 from **Advanced** and **Settings**.

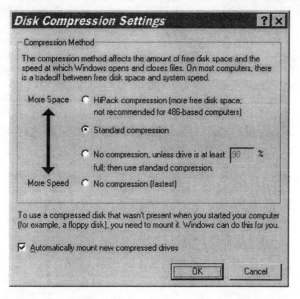

This shows that the more you try to claim extra disc space by using higher compression, the greater the performance penalty. In DriveSpace 3 the options are to select No Compression, Standard or HiPack compression. You may also select not to use compression at all unless the disc is 90% full. (This is the default figure and is adjustable by the user).

The next section looks at Compression Agent, another program within Microsoft Plus!, which has additional features for optimising the compression of discs. Compression Agent also provides UltraPack, a greater level of compression not available in DriveSpace 3.

Compression Agent

This is a component of Microsoft Plus! which can be scheduled (weekly, say) using the System Agent feature. It can also be run from the **System Tools** in the **Accessories** menu.

Compression Agent works to optimise speed and disc free space. Files which are not accessed regularly (e.g. in the last 30 days or whatever figure you specify) will be compressed using UltraPack, the highest level of compression.

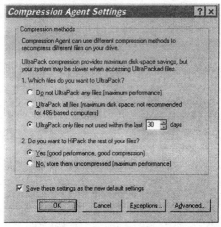

Recently used files are uncompressed or saved at a lower level of compression such as HiPack or Standard, to improve performance. This feature can be aborted if disc free space gets dangerously low. (The default is less than 20 MB - adjustable by the user).

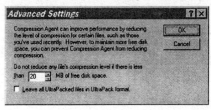

Summary: File and Disc Compression

- Files may be compressed to a fraction of their original size, depending on the type of data. Disc capacities may be more than doubled.

- File compression works by converting common words, etc, to a shorter than normal code.

- A .ZIP archive file is created which acts as a folder for compressed files. Files can be compressed by "dragging" and "dropping" them onto the .ZIP file.

- Files must be uncompressed or extracted before they can be used as normal files in applications.

- Special self-extracting files can be created in programs like PKZIP or WinZip. These have the .EXE extension and "unzip" themselves when you double-click on their file name. Self-extracting .EXE files are useful for sending compressed files to people who don't have an "unzip" program.

- File compression is very efficient for backing up files onto floppy disc, for distribution purposes.

- .ZIP compressed files are a fast and efficient vehicle for sending data around a network, including the Internet. The WinZip Wizard simplifies the extraction of software downloaded from the Internet, as well as installing the software on your hard disc, ready to run.

- Disc compression is useful if you are struggling for hard disc space. DriveSpace 3 and Compression Agent are designed to manage and optimise the trade-off between free disc space and system speed. High compression ratios mean lower speed.

10. COMPUTER VIRUSES

What is a Virus?

A virus is a small computer program written to cause damage to software and data and inconvenience to the user. The virus enters a computer system insidiously (often from a floppy disc). If not detected the virus replicates and spreads throughout a hard disc; some viruses may only cause trivial damage - such as displaying a 'humorous' message - while others can destroy files or wipe an entire hard disc.

Even when a virus doesn't do any serious damage to files and software, the time spent in eradicating it is likely to be considerable - not to mention the anxiety caused to the user whose work is interrupted, possibly for several hours. Writing viruses is an act of vandalism which has already resulted in at least one prison sentence. The virus writers are invariably young men, presumably seeing the task as a challenge to their programming skills. Viruses can be bought commercially and it's even possible to buy 'virus authoring' software to assist in their production.

Viruses exist on floppy and hard discs. They can also reside temporarily in the computer's memory - but they are removed when the computer is switched off. Viruses do not permanently damage the physical components of the computer - the hardware such as the memory or printer.

Floppy discs are a major source of virus infection, but viruses can also enter your system via a modem from the Internet, e-mail or bulletin boards.

Types of Virus

The File Virus

These viruses attach themselves to program or executable files. These files are part of your applications software packages such as Word 6 or Excel 5. The file virus will not infect the documents or spreadsheets produced using the software.

The Macro Virus

A newer type of virus has been developed which infects the documents produced using programs such as Word and Excel. Such programs have their own inbuilt programming language. This allows the advanced user to write macros, or small routines for automating groups of frequently used instructions. Unfortunately the virus writers have found ways of writing viruses in the macro language. Now even Word documents and Excel spreadsheets are vulnerable to virus attack. So it is possible for your hard disc to be infected with viruses spread in document files received via the Internet or e-mail (as well as files transferred from floppy disc).

Boot Sector Viruses

This is the most common type of virus. The boot sector is an area of a floppy or hard disc and contains information needed when the computer is started up or "booted". Even a floppy disc containing only data files has a boot sector which can be infected by a virus. If this apparently harmless disc is inadvertently left in a floppy disc drive when the computer is switched off, next time the machine is "booted", the virus can spread via the memory to the hard disc.

There are many ways in which the virus writer tries to cause damage whilst avoiding detection. The stealth virus actively tries to conceal itself by making the computer behave normally until it's ready to strike.

The Trojan, as its name implies, is a program with an apparently genuine function, which is really designed to do damage. It is not a virus since it does not replicate itself. Logic Bombs and Time Bombs are types of Trojan which are triggered when a certain event or date occurs.

The Polymorphic Virus changes its identity every time it replicates; it does this by repeatedly encrypting or encoding itself.

At the time of writing there are over 13,000 known viruses, each with a name, usually given by the anti-virus companies or the virus writers themselves.

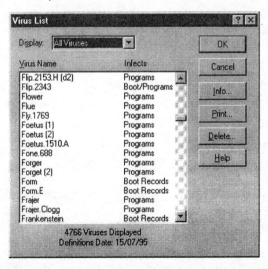

Each of these known viruses has a set of recognizable characteristics which the main anti-virus packages can detect.

Anti-Virus Software

The last ten years has seen the evolution of an ever-increasing list of computer viruses. At the same time, major companies have developed anti-virus software to detect and eradicate viruses. Two of the leading software packages are Norton AntiVirus and Dr. Solomon's Anti-Virus Toolkit.

The anti-virus software must not only find and destroy the existing base of many thousands of known viruses - it must also recognize 'virus-like activity,' possibly caused by new and unknown viruses. Virus-like activity would include the computer trying to alter program files - this shouldn't happen during the normal operation of the computer.

The main functions of anti-virus software are therefore:

- To continually monitor the memory and vulnerable files, to prevent viruses entering the hard disc and spreading to cause havoc and destruction.

- To allow the user to carry out manual scans to check the memory, floppy and hard discs, whenever required.

- To allow the automatic scheduling of scans, e.g. at a certain time each day or weekly.

- To remove viruses and repair infected files.

The complete anti-virus software is permanently installed on the hard disc. In addition, should the hard disc become severely infected, a floppy disc containing the main virus repair program should also be available.

Features of Anti-Virus Software

When you buy a complete anti-virus package such as Dr. Solomon's Anti-Virus Toolkit or Norton AntiVirus, the package will comprise a suite of programs which provide 3 different modes of scanning:

1. A scan available from the Windows 95 menus, like any other piece of software. This will be referred to as a Manual Scan in the following sections.

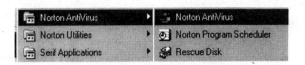

2. A scheduled scan, set up to run automatically at pre-set times.

3. A memory resident scan, which is permanently running in the background.

1.The Manual Scan

This is the main scanning program invoked from the Windows 95 program menu. (It can also be programmed to run automatically every time the computer starts up). The user can select this scan whenever they wish to check the hard disc or a newly acquired floppy disc. This scanner also allows the repair of files containing viruses.

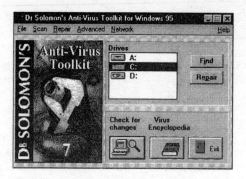

As can be seen above, there is an option to display the Virus Encyclopedia - a list of all currently known viruses.

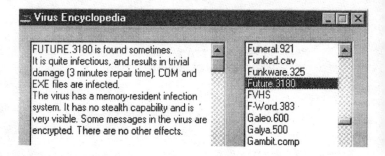

Since there are new viruses discovered every day, the anti-virus software should be updated monthly or quarterly to remain effective.

To initiate a scan, the user selects the required drive (usually A: or C:). If the check is successful i.e. no virus is found, the following screen is displayed:

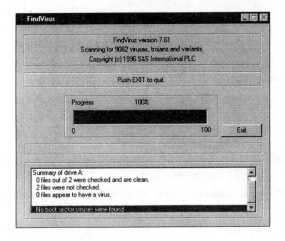

Detecting Unknown Viruses

In addition to the existing "catalogue" of known viruses, the anti-virus software should also detect unknown viruses. This is achieved by logging the details of files when they are known to be virus free. These details, such as the file size, are known as "fingerprints" and are recorded in a special file. When the user's files are scanned, the details of the files are compared with the original "fingerprint". A virus attaching itself to a program file will increase the size of the file. Since program files do not change in size in normal usage, any increase in size from the fingerprint indicates possible virus infection.

In Norton AntiVirus, the process of creating the "fingerprint" file is known as inoculation.

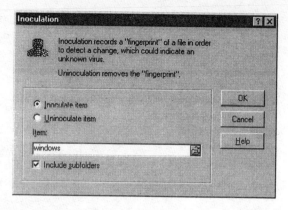

Although program files should not change in normal use, there are times when changes will genuinely occur, such as when the software is upgraded to a new version. To prevent this legitimate activity triggering false virus alarms, there is an option to remove the inoculation temporarily to allow the upgrade to take place. After the upgrade, the modified files/directories should be inoculated again.

2. Scheduled Scans

The previous section described the manual scan, selected from a menu whenever required by the user. In order to automate this process, packages such as Norton Anti-Virus include a Program Scheduler. This allows any program, such as a virus scanner, to be run at a pre-set time and frequency, e.g. daily, weekly or monthly.

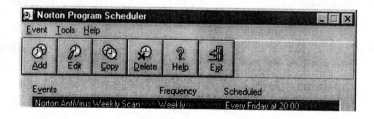

An advantage of the scheduled scan is that it removes from the user some of the responsibility for regular virus checking - although you should continue to carry out manual scans as well, particularly on newly-acquired floppy discs.

If you are using the computer when a scan is scheduled, you can carry on working while the scan continues in the background; a report on the scan appears on the screen when the scan is completed. If the computer happens to be switched off at the time of the scheduled scan, a report will appear next time you switch on to say that the scan was cancelled.

3. The Memory Resident Scanner (TSR)

This type of scanner is an example of a Terminate and Stay Resident Program (TSR). These are permanently loaded in the computer's memory and ready to run - unlike the manual scanner which has to be loaded into memory off the hard disc every time you select it from the menus.

The TSR scanner is loaded into memory when the computer starts up. It remains in the memory until the computer is switched off. The TSR scanner works constantly in the background monitoring the system for viruses, while the user continues with their normal work.

An example of a TSR program is the Auto-Protect facility (part of Norton Anti-Virus). The dialogue box **Auto Protect Settings** is shown on the next page.

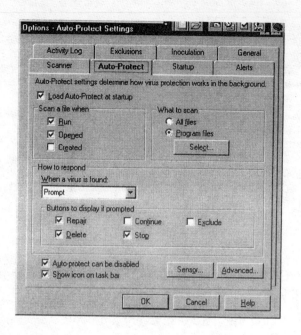

When you start the computer, the TSR scanner checks the memory and the system files for viruses. Then, while you are using the computer, this memory resident scanner checks all of the programs and files which you attempt to use. This is a constant monitoring process; if a virus is found, a warning message appears and you are prevented from using the infected file.

The memory resident scanners are limited in size by their need to reside permanently in memory. So they may not have the full range of features of the main menu-driven scanners. For example, it may not be possible to carry out the repair of infected files using the memory resident scanner.

If a Virus Strikes

If you are unfortunate enough to suffer a virus infection, a warning message will appear on the screen, accompanied by an alarm sound.

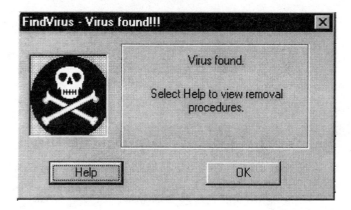

There are several locations in which a virus may be discovered:

- In the memory of the computer.

- In the boot or partition sector of a hard disc.

- In a file on hard or floppy disc or in the boot sector of a floppy disc.

1. The Virus in Memory

This is an extremely dangerous situation, since the virus is ideally placed to damage any files which are run or accessed from hard or floppy disc.

On finding a virus in memory:

- Shut down the computer immediately, using the correct procedure.

- Switch off the power to the computer. (This will remove the virus from memory).

- Re-start the computer using a write-protected floppy boot disc (which must be known to be free from viruses.)

- Packages such as Norton AntiVirus and Dr Solomon's Anti-Virus Toolkit include a diskette version of the virus detection/repair program. Use the floppy disc version of the anti-virus software to find and repair any viruses on the hard disc.

2. The Virus in the Boot or Partition Sector of a Hard Disc

As for a virus discovered in memory, the computer must be shut down and switched off immediately. After booting from a clean, write-protected disc, the anti-virus program is run from a floppy. If a virus is found in the boot sector of the hard disc, the boot sector is replaced by a clean boot sector which is generated by the software, after analysing your hard disc.

3. A Virus in a File on a Hard or Floppy Disc or in the Boot Sector of a Floppy Disc.

It should be possible to eradicate these viruses using the repair option on the manually selected scanner running from the hard disc, i.e. without shutting down and re-booting from a clean floppy as in cases 1 and 2.

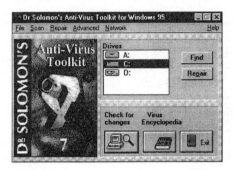

Repairing Files

Selecting the repair option should allow any infected files to be either repaired or renamed or removed. The program informs you when the repair has been completed.

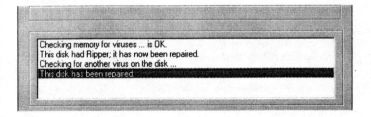

If a file cannot be repaired, it must be either re-named or deleted. Since a virus is really a program itself, it can be eradicated by deleting the infected file and replacing with a "clean" copy. If an infected floppy disc cannot be repaired it should be re-formatted.

Infected Floppy Discs

If it is suspected that a large number of floppy discs may be infected, they must all be checked and repaired using the main scanning program. In a business, this could be a massive task requiring the allocation of considerable time.

If a New Virus is Discovered

If your software has detected a possible virus, but cannot find it within its list of virus definitions, contact the supplier of your anti-virus software for more information and possible help.

Summary - Computer Viruses

* Obtain an established anti-virus package such as Norton AntiVirus or Dr. Solomon's Anti-Virus Toolkit.

* Install the anti-virus software on your hard disc, configured to provide scans :

    1. automatically on startup.

    2. continually while the computer is running.

    3. manually when selected with the mouse.

    4. automatically at regular scheduled times.

- Obtain and install regular software upgrades so that the virus definition list is always up-to-date with the latest known viruses.

- Always run a manual check on all floppy discs acquired from elsewhere. Be extremely sceptical about all diskettes - even packaged software from reputable companies has been known to be infected.

- Carry out regular manual or scheduled checks on all hard and floppy discs.

- Be vigilant when other people use the computer - insist that any diskettes are scanned before use. Formatting will remove viruses from a floppy disc.

- Make sure you have a clean, i.e. virus free, write-protected boot disc which will allow you to start the computer after a virus attack. A copy of a virus scanner on floppy disc, such as Dr. Solomon's Magic Bullet, is essential for situations where the hard disc is too infected to use.

- Make backup copies of important files when you know they are clean. An infected file can be repaired by overwriting with a clean version.

- "Booting up" or starting from an infected floppy disc accidentally left in the drive is a common entry route for viruses. Set your computer to boot by reading from the hard disc, without looking at the floppy disc. (If necessary, your local computer "expert" should be able to set this up in no time at all).

- Increasing use of the Internet is providing greater opportunities for the virus writers to create havoc. Always carry out a virus check on all files downloaded from the Internet or received as e-mail.

INDEX

NOTES